With Thanks to SUPERMAN:
40 Years of Interviews, Reports, and Observations

Brian McKernan

Parrville Press
Rye, New York

BRIAN MCKERNAN

ISBN: 979-8-218-05811-1

Cover design by Scott and Minky Billups. "Streaking" title typography by Aaron Price. Photo by Elizabeth P. McKernan. Star field by The NASA James Webb Space Telescope.
Cover Image credit: NASA, ESA, CSA, and STScI

SUPERMAN created by Jerry Siegel and Joe Shuster

All photos are by the author unless otherwise indicated.

Email: BrianMcKernanVO@outlook.com

The Parrville Press

Rye, New York

BRIAN MCKERNAN

Contents

BRIAN MCKERNAN

Acknowledgements

To my late sister Rita M. Gosman's friend (I'm sorry I forgot your name), who gave me a stack of DC comics when I had a summertime flu, circa 1959. To my parents and siblings, who "gave-in" to the pleadings of the youngest member of the household and let me watch *The Adventures of Superman* even when it was opposite *The Huntley–Brinkley Report*. To my wife and daughter, who patiently tolerate my Superman obsession.

To friend and novelist Steven Schindler, who told me to write *this* book so many times I finally did it. To Elizabeth P. McKernan, for the cover photo and so much more. To Scott and Minky Billups of The Pixelmonger Empire, for their Super cover design and crucial technical advice. To Aaron Price, for his Super cover typography. To Caped Wonder creator Jim Bowers, for the opportunity for me to say that this is the *second* book I have written about Superman. To Chuck Harter and Steve McCracken, for an unforgettable *Holiday in Metropolis*. To Toni VallesKey Collins, for being an ally in the never-ending battle to publicize Bob Holiday's rightful place in live-action Superman history. To Jim Nolt, who enables The Adventures to Continue. To Jim Hambrick, for more than I can say here. To Danny Fuchs, for the same reason. To Morgan and Adam Siebert, for making The Super Museum better every day. To former employer and novelist Robert Lipkowitz, for the title of this book, for his encouragement, and much more.

To all the great folks I've met over the years that share my fascination with the "strange visitor from another planet with powers and abilities far beyond those of mortal men." To the hundreds of writers, editors, artists, producers, directors, actors, and technicians who repeatedly made us all believe a man could fly, whether in the pages of a ten-cent comic book or on a $100 million movie screen.

And to Jerry Siegel and Joe Shuster, who started it all.

Chapter One

Introduction

Just what the world needs right now: another Superman book.

In the last few years Superman and his spandex-clad colleagues have inspired scores of books, including essay collections packed with the kind of detail and analysis once reserved for corporate titans and heads of state. Add to that the many superhero biographies, novels, film books, comic reprints, and self-help guides, and it's clear that these four-color fantasy figures have become role models and opinion leaders. Is that a good thing? Perhaps it's inevitable in an age when our putative leaders consistently disappoint.

Superheroes are big business today, as evidenced by all the blockbuster movies and slick TV shows made possible by advanced digital imaging solutions. In reality, however, all of those characters are the progeny of Superman, widely recognized as the first modern superhero. The ultimate wish-fulfillment figure, possessing amazing powers and the freedom of flight, Superman has been copied endlessly since his 1938 debut, with each new version (Captain Marvel, Captain America, Spider-Man) a remix of the original concept. In fact most, perhaps all, of these super-competitors currently overshadow Superman, who is apparently too heroic and uncomplicated to satisfy modern audience appetites for cynicism and irony. Yet Superman's presence in popular culture goes far beyond whoever's headlining at your local megaplex. Superman's fame has been pervasive for the better part of the past century. His appeal is deeply rooted in every Clark Kent's private belief that there's a

Superman dwelling deep within them. Small wonder, then, that this latest version of Gilgamesh is also a frequent go-to guy for the mass media.

Consider: Environmental activist Erin Brockovich recently published a study of the looming crisis in America's fresh-water supply. She could have given her book any number of titles, but she named it ***Superman's Not Coming***. Screenwriter J. Michael Straczynski's 2019 autobiography detailing his journey from childhood poverty to Hollywood triumph cites the main inspiration for his success in the book's title, ***Becoming Superman***. State representative Bruce Franks Jr. from St. Louis is the subject of the 2019 documentary ***St. Louis Superman*** about his fight for equality in Ferguson, Missouri. ***We Are Superman*** is another documentary; made in 2012 it details challenges in the Troost Avenue neighborhood of Kansas City. ***Sunshine Superman***, meanwhile, was not only a chart-topping Sixties pop tune from folk singer Donovan Leitch, it was also the title of a 2008 documentary about him and a 2014 documentary depicting the life and death of Carl Boenish, the American father of free-fall "BASE jumping." Then there was educator and social activist Geoffrey Canada's controversial 2010 documentary film about America's public education system, ***Waiting For Superman***. Seems like a trend. But it's nothing new for Superman. He's been a ready reference for a long time.

First, why this book? It's the least I can do to thank Superman for giving us all a welcome emotional lift from time to time. The book exists because—like millions of so-called *boomers*—I've been fascinated with this character for as long as I can remember. This fascination originated as a child reading Superman's comic book exploits and seeing actor George Reeves portray him on television. Perhaps that's why I not only chose journalism as a career, but journalism that covered television and movie production technology. During the past 40 years that decision has occasionally given me opportunities to write articles about Superman's long multimedia history for a variety of outlets. This book is a collection of most of those articles, updated and expanded to include additional information. A few other chapters were written specifically for this volume. Over the years I have also been amazed by Superman's status as multimedia, pop-culture icon. He's so firmly embedded in the public consciousness that he's referenced with startling regularity in the mass media and advertising. Keep your eyes peeled for these references in your local newspaper; they're there.

As I write this, the latest issue of *Psychology Today* (April 2022) features a Superman-inspired cover, a Superman-inspired ad graphic on its back cover, and two unrelated Superman-derived illustrations inside the issue. I don't believe there's any other fictional character quite so familiar and capable of communicating so much information at a glance. I even created a Facebook group—Superman in Advertising & Media—to document this curious fact. And as a journalist and PR writer, I found inspiration in the character's dual role as reporter Clark Kent and Superman. He's definitely an alter ego and someone we all wish would occasionally visit our troubled world.

This book is not, however, a comprehensive history of Superman. Other writers have already published those, the best of them being Larry Tye's *Superman: The High-Flying History of America's Most Enduring Hero* (Random House, 2012), which I strongly recommend. There's an annotated bibliography at the end of the book you're currently holding in your hands listing many other titles on Superman-related topics that are also worth your time. But first, let's consider why Superman occupies such a unique position.

German philosopher Friedrich Nietzsche is said to have originated the term *Übermensch* (**Superman**) for his very different 1885 concept of an amoral, dispassionate superior being. The Superman created in 1935 by impoverished Cleveland teenagers Jerry Siegel and Joe Shuster, however, turned this concept on its head with a genuine *mensch*—one that can also fly. Superman's 1938 *Action Comics* debut resonated with a Depression-weary, war-fearing public. Kids at the magazine racks of their local candy stores were the first to be amazed by Superman, but their parents soon picked-up on the character in 1939, when he began appearing in what would eventually total more than 300 daily newspapers (back when people actually read newspapers). Parents could hardly miss their children listening to Superman's nationwide radio serial, starting in 1940. And theatergoers of all ages saw the first of 17 brilliant-Technicolor Fleischer/Famous Studios Superman cartoon shorts at the movies starting in 1941.

Superman was the living embodiment of fearlessness and heroism just when the public needed him most. Hitler's 1937 terror-inducing blitzkrieg of the Spanish city of Guernica was still a vivid memory when Superman came on the scene. Killing an estimated 1,600 civilians, the event was immortalized in Picasso's famous horizontally shaped comic-strip-like painting. Guernica made everyone aware that they weren't even safe in their towering modern cities, which is probably why Metropolis (a name borrowed from German director Fritz Lang's 1927 expressionist science-fiction film) has always been so integral to the Superman mythos. The Man of Steel is every American city's reassuring guardian, a modern-day angel with wings sublimated into a flowing red cape. When war came copies of Superman comic books were in the backpacks of countless GI's. His image was painted on the noses of U.S. warplanes. Superman newspaper strips, radio episodes, and theatrical cartoons all had him helping with the war effort.

Despite being a preposterous fantasy-figure, Superman's mass appeal was quickly evidenced in the popular culture. He inspired creative minds. Benny Goodman recorded a "Superman" jazz instrumental written by arranger Eddie Sauter in 1940. Superman was suddenly being name-checked in Hollywood movies, including *All Through the Night* (1941), *A-Haunting We Will Go* (1942), *So Proudly We Hail* (1943), *No Time For Love* (1943), and *Once Upon a Time* (1944). Rather amazing for a character that didn't even exist just a few years earlier. The trend continued after the war. Trumpeter Pete Candoli penned an original composition titled "Superman" in 1946 and wore a Superman costume onstage whenever he performed the song as a member of Woody Herman's band. The Miles Davis Quintet recorded its own "Superman" instrumental in 1947, written by Davis himself. Fast-forward to today, and the list of Superman-inspired melodies numbers more than 100, encompassing nearly every musical genre and acts ranging from Barbra Streisand to Eminem (see Chapter Fifteen).

The public's fascination with The Man of Steel, as he became known, soon led to his use in advertising. Popular newspaper-strip characters such as The Yellow Kid, Buster Brown, and Jiggs & Maggie had paved the way years earlier, successfully selling everything from cigarettes to corned beef and cabbage. Just a few months after Superman's debut, enterprising National (DC) Comics owners Harry Donenfeld and Jack Liebowitz created Superman, Inc. as a business entity to license Superman to sell Kellogg's cereals, Ogilvie oats, Conoco gasoline, Dan River dresses, and several brands of bread. They also authorized the Superman-TIM Club, a nationwide franchise for department stores and independent haberdashers designed to make clothes shopping more appealing to boys (and less challenging for parents and merchants). Club members received Superman-TIM "redback" play money (redeemable for banners, buttons, pencils, and other premiums) and the monthly *Superman-Tim* newsletter, which included stories, puzzles, jokes, contests, and tips on good citizenship. This Man of Steel was solid gold.

Superman wasn't the only attraction for juveniles that became a multimedia sensation in comics, on radio, in movie serials, and early TV. But unlike such contemporaries as The Lone Ranger, Flash Gordon, and Zorro, he's still appearing in movies and currently headlines *Superman and Lois*, a live-action TV series (his fifth since 1952) on the CW network. It's hardly a kids' show, focusing on the titular characters' struggles to balance raising two teenage boys with work, societal pressures, and diabolical adversaries. But Superman has appealed to thinking adults for some time.

A recently discovered risqué poem written in 1942 by *Lolita* novelist Vladimir Nabokov pondered Superman's intimacy issues. Canadian media-studies guru Marshall McLuhan's 1951 pop-culture study *The Mechanical Bride* included a harsh critique of Superman. "Superman and Paula Brown's New Snowsuit" was a 1955 short story about childhood disillusionment by poet and novelist Sylvia Plath. *Murder By Contract*, a

1958 film noir cited as a major influence on director Martin Scorsese, features a gangster (Phillip Pine) repeatedly taunting an unsuccessful hitman (Vince Edwards) by calling him Superman. Tennessee Williams' decidedly adult 1960 play *Period of Adjustment* and its subsequent film version make Superman a central theme in a young veteran's PTSD. Novelist Norman Mailer's *Esquire* magazine coverage of that year's presidential campaign of John F. Kennedy was titled *Superman Comes to the Supermarket*, based on Mailer's observation that the charismatic young candidate was being advertised like a household product. A few years later pop artists such as Andy Warhol and Roy Lichtenstein turned Superman comic book panels into million-dollar paintings sold by leading art dealers, and figurative painters such as Mel Ramos chose Superman as a serious subject for capturing on canvas. Many other artists have continued this trend, including Enrique Chagoya, Katherine Bradford, Llyn Foulkes, and Roger Shimomura. John Lennon, meanwhile, chose to wear a Superman T-shirt on the cover of his Penguin paperback. And then there's Laurie Anderson's *O Superman*, an eight-minute avant-garde phonograph record released in 1981 that charted in multiple countries.

Superman's role as an advertising pitchman, meanwhile, went into high gear in the 1960's when Liebowitz's nephew Jay Emmett co-founded The Licensing Corporation of America to officially authorize ads based on Superman and other DC character merchandise. They hit the jackpot when Batman's live-action 1966 ABC-TV series debuted, unleashing a bonanza of toys and other products. The LCA was so good at what it did it was soon handling everything from James Bond 007 to Major League Baseball. Emmett became a top VP at Warner Communications after its corporate antecedent bought DC in 1967. Buoyed by Superman's instant recognition factor, the character went on to advertise everything from Volkswagen buses to AT&T long-distance services. He appeared in magazine ads for Continental Insurance, *Newsweek* magazine, International Paper, U.S. Air Force recruiting, Diet Coke, Duracell batteries, Lands' End clothing, Lotus Notes, and in TV commercials for American Express cards with noted Superman fan Jerry Seinfeld. Overseas, Superman advertised German car batteries, Japanese coffee

The reigning superhero of advertising and media

makers, Argentine eyewear, British cosmetics, Indian polio vaccinations, Russian replacement windows, and even Iranian banking services.

Beyond the officially licensed use of Superman in advertising is the even more interesting realm of Superman as an at-a-glance symbol for power and prestige. When *Newsweek* profiled secretary of state Henry Kissinger in 1974, its cover depicted him as Superman, flying above the world. Three years later U.S. energy secretary James Schlesinger appeared on the cover of *Time* in a blue Superman leotard and red cape clutching a lightning bolt. *The Economist* similarly caricatured the U.S. economy as Superman with a dollar sign on his chest in 1985. *The Week* featured billionaire Mike Bloomberg as Superman on a 2019 cover. And these weren't the only occasions when each of these magazines featured Superman-inspired cover illustrations.

Even more common are ads and magazine covers inspired by Christopher Reeve's shirt-open scene in 1978's *Superman: The Movie* as he ran toward the camera revealing the big red S on his chest before zooming skyward to save Lois Lane dangling from a helicopter. The "shirt-open" motif was later applied to such famous folks as Margaret Thatcher (*National Review*), Mitt Romney (*The Week*), Barrack Obama (*Ms.*), P. Diddy (*Vibe*), lifestyle guru Tim Ferris (*Outside*), quarterback Cam Newton (*GQ*), and many others.

And then there's the Superman's "litany," written in 1941 by artist Jay Morton for the first Fleischer Superman cartoon and re-used to intro each episode of the 1950s *Adventures of Superman* TV series: *"Faster than a speeding bullet, more powerful than a locomotive, able to leap tall buildings in a single bound! Look! Up in the sky! It's a bird...it's a plane...it's Superman!"* Today these words are known to all, and are frequently paraphrased in newspaper and magazine headlines and captions, and in advertisements. And don't forget such tried-and-true as phrases as "This looks like a job for...," "Up, up, and away...," and clichés involving X-ray vision, telephone booths, kryptonite, "bizarro," etc. All have been used in instant-recognition ads so familiar they don't require a second thought. Be on the lookout. You'll see them.

It's all rather remarkable for an improbable, imaginary hero born in the pages of a ten-cent comic book (early pristine copies of which now sell for in excess of $3 million). And that's why I decided he merits yet another book, albeit one from my personal media-oriented perspective. I also have another perspective on the character, one that's almost spooky at times. I call it the *strange coincidences* perspective (or perhaps it's just a series of examples of my own "confirmation bias," the tendency to interpret events as confirmation of one's interests).

I'll share a few: I had a high school classmate who went on to become a famous Superman comic book artist; another classmate's brother played Superboy on television years later; I worked at a magazine in 1979 that occupied offices just vacated by Superman publisher DC Comics; another office included two co-workers who were cousins of the actors that played Supergirl and Superboy (and were quite surprised when I told them that); a 2003 phone offer to co-produce a Superman documentary was "decided" for me moments later when someone coincidentally dropped an autographed Superman photo on my desk; a chance conversation at my barber provided a lead on obtaining a copy of a "lost" Superman TV commercial; a fellow bus-rider returning from a broadcast technology conference spontaneously informed me he was a Superman fan (and he was from Indonesia); an interview assignment in Washington DC coincided with an opportunity to visit the Smithsonian's 1988 Superman exhibit; an after-dinner stroll near a co-worker's Santa Monica CA apartment led me right to a movie theater that had appeared in a Superman-related television pilot filmed decades earlier; and I walked past Christopher Reeve on Columbus Avenue one morning in 1985 on my way to work. I'd have said hello, but he was deep in conversation with someone. And that was fine by me; we had spoken on the phone just two years earlier (see Chapter Three).

Confirmation bias, perhaps, but I suspect the Universe is nudging me to acknowledge that Siegel and Shuster's popular character may have underlying layers of significance that differentiate him from all the other Hallmark card inspirations. What they are, I have not yet figured out. Have you? In any case, I have assembled this compilation of 40 years' worth of Superman reports, interviews, and reflections. I hope you'll enjoy reading them as much as I did writing them.

Brian McKernan, 2022.

Chapter Two

The Supermen

Before I write another word, I need to acknowledge four remarkable men who deserve mention for their super-heroic contributions to preserving Superman's history and building avid communities of super-interest.

Three of them are named Jim and one is named Danny. Let's start with the Jims. I believe these three met jointly on only one occasion (the 2016 Metropolis IL memorial service for Noel Neill, Lois Lane of serials and television), but their individual efforts on behalf of saving and preserving historic Superman artifacts and building communities of interest should earn each of them a bright red cape.

The first is **Jim Hambrick**, originally a Californian who began collecting Superman memorabilia more than 60 years ago when he was six years old. His mother's gift of a Superman lunchbox during a lengthy hospital stay launched him on a remarkable journey that would turn his childhood fascination into a lifetime career as the man who established The Super Museum in Metropolis IL, the centerpiece of that community's annual Superman Celebration.

Hambrick learned early on that his classmates would gladly pay him a nickel to view his Superman toy collection. As he matured, he reached out to the producers, crew, and surviving cast of *The Adventures of Superman* series, one of the most successful film-originated shows in television syndication history. Rare costumes, scripts, and props that would have been discarded were passed along to Hambrick for preservation, and he became friends with several of the show's actors and effects wizards. These friendships led to his becoming the manager of actor Kirk Alyn, star of the 1948 and 1950 Superman movie serials.

At the same time nearly 2,000 miles away, local Metropolis IL businessman Bob Westerfield lobbied for his small, historic city of 6,500 on the banks of the Ohio River to capitalize on its unique name. His efforts prompted the Illinois State Legislature to pass Resolution 572 on June 9, 1972, which declared Metropolis to be "The Hometown of Superman." Superman owners DC Comics agreed, and a yearly Superman Celebration commenced each June. The 1978 release of *Superman: The Movie* greatly heightened interest in the initiative. Hambrick eventually packed up his tremendous Superman collection in a fleet of semis and moved it nearly 2,000 miles from Southern California to the center of Metropolis. There, just down the street from an impressive 15-ft. bronze Superman statue, he opened The Super Museum. This repository of more than 70,000 rare Superman artifacts attracts visitors 365 days a year and has been reported on by media from all over the world.

Every year during the second weekend in June, tens of thousands of visitors gather in Metropolis for the Superman Celebration, where celebrity guests—including actors from Superman-related movies and television shows, and leading comic book artists—sign autographs, participate in Q&A's with fans, and pose for photos. Cosplayers, meanwhile, show off amazing costumes, musical talents entertain, athletic events are held, classic cars are displayed, specialty food vendors and memorabilia pop-ups line the streets, and other family-oriented activities ensure a super-time for all ages.

Hambrick's life work of locating, acquiring, restoring, and displaying unique, diverse, and irreplaceable Superman costumes, props, photographs, toys, and other artifacts has reinforced the character's fame and provided countless numbers of families with a fun destination to feed their sense of super-wonder. He's been a consultant on Superman film projects, has helped promote Superman movies, and has been interviewed by scores of print and broadcast media outlets. His lifelong passion for all things Superman has benefitted his adopted hometown, and provided a global destination for Superman aficionados.

Credit: Lisa Copenhaver

Jim Nolt (left) meets Jim Hambrick for the first time at the Metropolis IL Super Museum, in 2016.

The second Jim is **Jim Nolt**, a retired Pennsylvania schoolteacher who— like millions of others—has been fascinated with the *Adventures of Superman* since childhood. Like Jim Hambrick, however, he did something about it. Encouraged by the 1976 publication of author Gary Grossman's book *Superman: Serial to Cereal* (the first book-length history of the Superman movie serials and the Kellogg's-sponsored *Adventures of Superman* television series), he became a proactive fan. Nolt realized that his Superman-loving generation had come of age after seeing a 1976 episode of Tom Snyder's *Tomorrow Show* on NBC featuring author Grossman, Kirk Alyn, and television cast members Noel Neill (Lois Lane), Jack Larson (Jimmy Olsen), and Robert Shayne (Inspector Henderson).

Nolt reached out to these cast members, who were glad to finally be appreciated for their work by adults. He assumed the editorship of a fanzine started by medical doctor Don Rhoden, titled *The Adventures Continue*, in 1989 and published issue numbers 3 to 16 until 2001, when he transitioned this content to jimnolt.com (he had begun this move seven years earlier). Both the print fanzine and the website provided enthusiasts with a forum to share cast and crew interviews, rare photos, and original research. Nolt also appeared on the television series *Unsolved Mysteries* to comment on the mysterious death of actor George Reeves, and he assisted fellow fan Armand Vaquer in coordinating a Los Angeles County Board of Supervisors "Superman Week" event in 2001 (a commemoration of the fiftieth anniversary of the *Adventures of Superman* television series, which ended each episode with the text "Made in Hollywood, USA"). He also helped organize the celebration of Noel Neill's 85th birthday in 2005 and provided commentary for *The Adventures of Superman* DVD release the following year.

Nolt's diligent networking and organizing efforts also included large "Adventures Continue" fan gatherings in New York in 2009, 2011, and 2015, Los Angeles in 2014 and 2018, and Sarasota in 2017. The 2014 event, called Super Celebration 2014, marked the 100th birthday of George Reeves and Superman creators Jerry Siegel and Joe Shuster, and was attended by Jack Larson and scores of other *Adventures of Superman* notables. See Chapter 13 for a full report on this event.

Jim Nolt's tireless efforts to preserve the memory of George Reeves and his fellow cast members continue on his jimnolt.com website and Adventures Continue Facebook page. Perhaps this is why references to Reeves seem to be on the increase in the popular press, as younger Superman fans discover the series' DVDs and Nolt's extensive online content detailing this historic series and the talents behind it.

The third Jim is **Jim Bowers**, former U.S. Army paratrooper, professional photographer, graphic designer/artist, preservationist, archivist, event organizer, and creator/editor of CapedWonder.com, a fan-based website created to celebrate Christopher Reeve's legacy as an actor, humanitarian, teacher, and family man. The site also honors film director Richard Donner and the other creative talents behind the four Reeve Superman movies. Bowers has worked for more than 30 years to research, gather, and restore rare photographs and other content from

Super Museum director Morgan Hambrick, founder Jim Hambrick, and Jim Bowers inspect a vintage George Reeves Superman costume, 2016.

these films, and to present them to fans and film historians on his website capedwonder.com and numerous social media platforms.

An active supporter of the Christopher & Dana Reeve Foundation, Bowers, along with Detroit television news anchor and morning radio host Jay Towers, also organized and moderated the 2015 Celebrity Super Reunion Q&A Panel at WonderCon Anaheim—the largest Christopher Reeve Superman celebrity reunion to date—and the Christopher Reeve Legacy Reunion at the Motor City Comic Con near Detroit in 2022. Both events featured multiple stars from the Reeve Superman films. Bowers and Towers, meanwhile, have recorded and posted more than 40 CapedWonder Superman podcasts with actors and crewmembers from these films, providing fascinating historical perspectives.

Bowers' other "super" credits include the full-color book *Superman: The Richard Donner Years, a Photographic Journey*. He also served as: research consultant for the three 2001 Warner Home Video *Superman: The Movie* Special Edition DVD documentaries; graphics/photography contributor to the 2006 *Superman Ultimate Collector's Edition* and *Christopher Reeve Superman Collection* DVD box sets; creative consultant and photographer for the 2008 *Superman-The Music (1978-1988)* eight-CD box set; and photography contributor to the 2008 *Special Effects Superman: The Art and Effects of Derek Meddings* coffee table book. He also contributed material to the 1998 DC Comics editions *Superman, The Complete History: The Life and Times of the Man of Steel* and *Superman Masterpiece Edition: The Golden Age of America's First Super Hero*; the 2010 Cinemaquette Superman booklet; Paul Levitz's 2010 book, *75 Years of DC Comics: The Art of Modern Mythmaking*; and Levitz's 2015 book, *The Little Book of Superman*. Bowers also served as creative consultant on La-La Land Records' *Superman IV* soundtrack CD set, *Superman II & Superman III* soundtrack CD set, and the *Superman: The Movie* soundtrack CD set. He also assisted with the 2021 Mondo *Superman: The Movie* soundtrack vinyl releases.

Danny Fuchs is often called "America's Foremost Superman Collector," and for good reason. Inspired during the early 1960s by *Superman* comic books and *The Adventures of Superman* television series, Fuchs became an avid collector of—and dealer in—rare Superman items, particularly extremely hard-to-find items from the 1940's. These include tin toys, games, coloring books, advertising ephemera, and premium items such as pin-back buttons and very rare Superman rings. He's also an expert on Superman figures, one of the most popular categories of Superman collectibles. The thousands of super-artifacts he has acquired during the past 60+ years include items that he loaned to the Smithsonian Institution's National Museum of American History for its 1987-88

Danny Fuchs (left) meets Jim Hambrick, at Nick at Nite's 1991 screening of *Superman and the Mole Men*, in New York.

Superman: Many Lives, Many Worlds exhibit. Fuchs was also the associate editor of *The Adventures of Superman Collecting* (Russ Cochran, 1988) the first book ever published to focus entirely and exclusively on the history, graphics, rarity, and value of Superman art and collectibles. Featuring more than 500 significant Superman items photographed in full color, this slipcase edition coffee table book was printed as a limited run of 2,500 copies.

Fuchs is retired now, but like his "colleagues named Jim" he's spent decades as a curator and archivist who has gone to great lengths to rescue one-of-a-kind Superman artifacts and vintage items from oblivion and has made them available to all to study and enjoy. He's also a very generous man.

There are other great Superman collectors out there besides these gentlemen, as well as enthusiasts, writers, and original content creators that space doesn't permit me to list. I know most of them only by reputation or an occasional Facebook post or comment. All, however, are "keepers of the flame" who have grown communities of super-appreciation and fellowship. Suffice it to say, every fan owes them a super-measure of gratitude.

Chapter Three

Interview with Christopher Reeve

Of all the actors who have portrayed Superman, Christopher Reeve gets my vote as the best. I grew up watching George Reeves on the *Adventures of Superman*, and will always love his earnest performances. Like Reeve, Reeves was an experienced stage and film actor and very serious about his craft. Another experienced Superman stage actor was Bob Holiday, star of the 1966 Hal Prince Broadway musical *"It's a Bird...It's a Plane...It's Superman."* Bob was a personal friend (see Chapter Eleven), which makes it even harder to pick a favorite. Nevertheless, Reeve gets my vote.

In 1983 I was a copy editor and writer at *Omni* magazine, a popular science journal featuring interviews with some of the world's best minds, including biologist E.O. Wilson, physicist Richard Feynman, and futurist Alvin Toffler. *Omni* also published work by the best names in science fiction, including *Game of Thrones* author George R.R. Martin, Isaac Asimov, Ray Bradbury, and many others. And *Omni* also reported on current cinema. When I learned in early 1983 that *Superman III* would be released that summer with an evil-computer subplot I knew I had to interview its star. Although we lived on the same Manhattan street on opposite sides of Central Park, Reeve was a challenge to connect with until I sent his secretary some powdered vitamin C for a bad cold she was suffering from. Reeve phoned me about an hour after the messenger delivered it to her office on March 15, 1983.

I found Reeve to be friendly, cooperative, and very much "on the same wavelength" as I, perhaps because we're about a year apart in age. What follows is an edited transcript to the original interview, large portions of which were used for my *Superman III* article in the August 1983 issue of *Omni* magazine (on newsstands that June). Ironically, neither of us had seen the film at the time of our interview. Also, at one point I asked Reeve if he owned a computer; bear in mind that most people didn't back then. Reeve was surprisingly candid, and this interview reflects that, with everyday colloquialisms spoken during this conversation. Reeve also tended to periodically rephrased his thoughts midway through his sentences. I have retained these features of the interview to accurately preserve the nature of my conversation with the first Superman of big-budget movies. I started the interview by explaining that *Omni* readers would be interested in the computer aspects of *Superman III*.

Reeve: I don't know how much I can tell you because I haven't seen the film. I'll do as much as I can within that framework if you have a deadline. It would be better—I'll be seeing the film probably in early April. Can you wait till then, or do you want to talk about things now?

McKernan: If I could talk now I'd appreciate it, because my deadline's April first.

Reeve: All right, okay.

McKernan: And the people at Warner Bros...can't tell me much about the plot or anything.

Reeve: Yeah, I have the same problem, but let me see how far we can take you.

McKernan: I know that there's computers in the film and our readership is interested in computers. In what sort of way are computers portrayed in the film?

Reeve: Ultimately, computers can be a destructive force that prevent people from relating to one another. Computers are misused in *Superman III* by certain bad elements, led by Robert Vaughn, who are trying to take over the world. They are abetted by the [Richard] Pryor character, who finally has a change of heart and eventually realizes that a high-tech, evil-minded scheme he's been led into is evil. Whether to stay with it or not is the moral choice he has to make, which way he's going to go.

McKernan: So, in other words, like any tool, the tool can be used or abused?

Reeve: Yeah. What happens with this film is whereas the other Superman films have started big and worked down. In other words, they've started in outer space, other planets, larger-than-life forces, the evil people who can fly, things like this. This film takes place right here in 1983, in this country with real, contemporary people who have a larger-than-life hero, Superman, in their midst. But we have no—no one else has super powers in this movie.

This movie literally starts on a matchbook cover and moves up into the world of technology; what happens if technology runs rampant. And Richard Pryor, literally, the opening shot in the movie is a guy is out of work in New York or wherever, and he picks up a matchbook cover that reads: EARN BIG MONEY, BE A COMPUTER PROGRAMMER—you know those things?—to light a cigarette, and it starts from there and works all the way up to a computer trying to take over the world. So you see the movie starting small and then opening up to the size of an epic-size movie.

McKernan: Do you own a personal computer?

Reeve: No. I have one of those calculators that I use. Generally I use it in the airplane to figure out ETA [expected time of arrival] of my next checkpoint or something, but other than that I don't use computers at all. And I hate video games.

McKernan: Yeah.

Reeve: Oh, I despise video games. I just think—when I look at people's faces, you know, sort of blue with the reflected light of some Atari game or something, it makes me sad. I'm sure it's fun for a while but it becomes a narcotic in a way.

McKernan: Yeah, they're like zombies or something.

Reeve: Yeah.

McKernan: Each film has shown us new aspects, new layers of the Clark/Superman personality. Will we see further aspects, new layers in *Superman III*?

Reeve: One of the changes you'll notice is that I back down a little bit on the physical comedy in Clark. He doesn't bump into walls quite so often. I feel that the audience will get bored with that by now. Also, Clark goes back to Smallville for his high-school reunion, and he makes a new friend. He meets this girl—played by Annette O'Toole—that he used to know when he was a kid, named Lana Lang. And she is now divorced and has a nine-year-old kid and is trying to make a living. Sort of a single mother now. Clark and Lana renew their friendship. In other words, she likes him and there's a kind of attraction, but it's not going to go any place. It's just friends, really.

And what happens is that—at the end of part two [*Superman II*] the romantic gesture at the end of part two where Superman causes Lois Lane to forget that they had the relationship, to forget that she knew him, that's the end of romance for Superman. The purity of it, I think, is important. That was his one true love and it didn't work out, and there won't be another. This idea that he sort of hops from bedroom to bedroom, you know, in contemporary fashion, I think is wrong.

So it's a friendship with Lana Lang in spite of however the studio or anyone else tries to pump it up into something else. And it's more important because it works. You know, when men and women aren't trying to impress each other something very close can develop. He sort of helps her without putting any pressure on and it's a very relaxed, friendly kind of thing. But she would not want to spend time with a nerd. If Clark is a real goofball, this classy, attractive girl would not want to spend time with him.

So I have made him, when he gets back to Kansas—and if you remember in the first movie when he grew up he was a perfectly normal farm kid with no behavioral problems at all. He didn't stutter and push his glasses around and stuff. But that was all a disguise he invented for living in the city. So when he goes back to Kansas we see him really drop all that and he sort of goes through a moment when he realizes "Why do I do all this shtick?"

So that's sort of new. You will see a far more normal Clark Kent without a lot of the mannerisms that go with it. So that's the new element in the character.

McKernan: You're not the first actor to portray Superman. In my opinion you're the best, and you probably won't be the last. I think of Bud Collyer, Kirk Alyn, George Reeves, Bob Holiday, but as the current "keeper of the flame," so to speak, do you have any thoughts like why Superman—who was created 50 years ago this June—is still so popular? Probably more popular now than he ever has been?

Reeve: Because he's such an accurate psychological model. And all the other heroes are basically derivative. They are some replica of Superman. You're combining basic fantasy with everyday reality, and it's an unbeatable combination. What person has not dreamt of flying and freedom and power and all those things, yet had to face the 9 to 5 work world that we all really live in?

Siegel and Shuster really made that—also with the use of the vivid colors, with the red, and the blue, and the yellow, very sort of harmonious colors symbolizing the things. It's a strong visual mass-media representation of something that goes on in every citizen of

Western culture, really. That sort of dilemma of "How do I function as an individual in a society where I feel like a mouse?"

In the 1930's—1933 particularly in the Depression—Siegel and Shuster said it first and best, I think. And all the other characters I think basically are some version of Superman. That's why. He was the first and the truest.

McKernan: I think that people sometimes wish there really was a Superman to get us out of, like somebody with an atom bomb in New York City. Somebody to really—

Reeve: I don't entertain those thoughts because I believe you shouldn't mix fantasy with the real world. It's a mistake. Superman should be left up on the screen or on the page or in people's minds. You shouldn't even bring him out into the daylight, so to speak. It just isn't fair.

McKernan: You've done such a terrific characterization of Superman, making him modern and believable. What was it like to suddenly have to play his antithesis? You know, the anti-Superman. The complete opposite of what he is?

Reeve: With that we're trying to not talk about. We're sort of leaving that for people to discover in the film.

McKernan: Okay.

Reeve: If someone has spilled it to you, they shouldn't have.

McKernan: Nobody did. I sort of deduced that this was the case. But that's a no-no, huh?

Reeve: It would be really nice, since your magazine is, you know, you could say it was a scoop, but it would really help us and the audience if you don't get into that.

McKernan: Okay. We wouldn't scoop the movie anyway because this issue's coming out at the same time the movie's released.

Reeve: Uh huh.

McKernan: I'm enough of a fan not to blow it.

Reeve: I think, yeah, there's a nice surprise coming for people. And let's leave it at that. If you want to do some follow-up material after the movie's out and then talk about it when it's become current and everyone knows the secret, then we can talk about it.

McKernan: *Omni* interviewed Terrence Stamp two years ago and he said that flying was sheer agony. But you always make it look so effortless and pleasant. Is it really that painful and everything?

Reeve: No, I don't think so. You have to prepare for it, but it's very easy. I mean, sometimes on location in Canada after I'd finish a shot we just take people, we'd take extras and put them up on the wires and whip 'em around, fly 'em around. If you were to put the flying equipment in an amusement park—the stuff that I use—and put it at Knott's Berry Farm or Magic Mountain—whatever these places are—people would queue up to go do it.

McKernan: Do you use one or two, several wires?

Reeve: Well, there's four or five different techniques. I guess we're not supposed to get into that. But it involves everything from wires to front projection to traveling matte, to blue screen, all that stuff.

McKernan: Richard Pryor on a recent *Tonight Show with Johnny Carson* told about you both being airborne and him being very scared because, I guess, it was one of his first times, and you're saying, "Hey, don't worry, I've got you." And he thought this was funny because he said, "What was I worrying about? I was with Superman?" Was that pretty much how it happened with that anecdote?

Reeve: Not only as Superman, but also as the actor, I know how to do that stuff. I was simply telling him [Pryor] that I had the stunt under control, that the wires were safe, that I've practiced it, that there's no problem, and I was sort of controlling what we were doing, and I was telling him "Don't worry, I've worked it out, and we're fine." But nothing, if there was a massive power failure and the crane were to break or the gears to slip, I'd go down like anybody else. I was not talking to him as Superman.

McKernan: I realize that. I'm not—that sounds like a cheap shot, that's not what I'm trying to say. I thought it was a funny anecdote that I could incorporate.

Reeve: Basically what they did was they scared him. They were afraid that he wouldn't want to do it. I rehearsed with him in the studio for a couple of days, taking him off the floor slowly, first three feet, then five feet, and then ten, and saying that this is what we do, and then we rotate, and then you get your feet ready, and then you land, and then you take it in your knees. Taking him through it.

But they got him on the set at eight in the morning and suddenly he was outside on a crane instead of the ceiling and they whipped him up to 60 feet without any preparation. They put the harness on, the wires, and suddenly he was up dangling in the air with a lot of people watching outdoors. And a crane looks very flimsy. These construction cranes look scary, they don't look solid.

It was just not a kind thing to do. They should have eased him into it. But since the scene called for him to be terrified anyway, the unit knew that he was perfectly safe and they decided to get that real fear. Dick Lester is big on that. No one was in danger at any time, but they could have been more courteous to Richard, I think.

McKernan: How was he on the set? I understand he's very spontaneous. I know that [director Richard] Lester uses multiple cameras. Did you do a lot of things in one take for spontaneity?

Reeve: Many things were one take but also Richard can be really fishing for two or three takes and then suddenly get it, whereas I tend to figure it out in rehearsal and then repeat it and refine it. You know, I'll figure out what I'm going to do in the rehearsal and then I'll try to make it better each time but not really changing it. So I'm trying to get more in the groove. But Richard doesn't do that. He's like a flat stone skipping over the water; it'll bounce four times before it goes in. And he's very interesting that way. That stone skipping is fun to watch, you know, and how many times it's going to bounce. That's actually a pretty good image for it. But you'd better be ready when he hits, is the point.

So as long as you stay alive and stay in tune, then when he gets the one take where it's all working, then both people meet. The danger is that you'll be off

Credit: Warner Bros.

Christopher Reeve and Richard Pryor balanced action and humor in *Superman III* (1983).

when he's on, 'cause he'll have done it two or three times, get tired of it, and then just suddenly find it. But it's like opening a box of Whitman Samplers. There's 48 flavors of candy in there and the problem is you like all the candy; it's hard to choose. So it's an excess of richness rather than of being too little.

McKernan: How was the combination of Pryor and Lester, Lester having done comedy too. Did it make for some pretty funny times?

Reeve: I remember them being polite and cordial, but no more than that. Richard Pryor came on to work and then go home. He would do his things, there would be a lot of laughs on the set but—no—it was not a nonstop party. It was professional, it was economical. Richard would come out, do the scene, and go away. There was not a lingering family feeling because that's not really what's encouraged there. We're moving so fast that when the shot's over everyone's mind is on the next thing. So, as opposed to [*Superman: The Movie* director] Dick Donner, who kind of luxuriated in each thing and then gradually let it go and then go on to the next thing, Lester's not that way. So Pryor picked up that style. I think he was probably more economical on this film than on any of the other things he's done. He got to the point quickly and many things were the first take, eventually.

McKernan: You've always taken Superman seriously. A lot of appropriate humor, but I'm curious with Pryor, is *Superman III* more of a comedy than the previous films?

Reeve: It's closer to [*Superman*] *II* than to *I* in style. More of a comic book, and I think that's right. We mustn't pump this up into being pseudomythology. It's really a comic book and within that we play it straight, but it's just that. It's two hours where you check your problems at the door. But we don't address the real world. I think that's cruel to say this is America in a literal way. What we do is in a more affectionate—I don't know.

The style with Lester is not just to spoof any values or anything, but to show absurdities in the world. And rather than—I mean the difference between that and, say, the box of Cheerios on the breakfast table and the unlimited horizon of wheat fields, and all that scene-painting that Dick Donner did in part one. Part three has much more the sort of Lester style to it.

McKernan: According a Mark McClure interview I read, he says you are the leader on the set, and if you don't want to do something it's not done. Were there any changes you made on this film?

Reeve: Oh sure, quite a lot, but that makes me sound out to be a bit of a dictator. This is all in a friendly way. No more [changes] than you would do working off-Broadway. I think that Superman is a character that I know. If I didn't know it I've been wasting six years. Often they will defer to my judgment because I know what I'm doing in this part and it just simply happens naturally.

They'll set something up and I'll say "I think he'd fly left to right, or he'd go low-level here, or he'd go up," whatever. I had much to do with the flying this time. I sort of oversaw a great deal of how the flying was to be done. Whereas in the first two films I kind of went for the ride. And I feel that the flying is...I don't know, I'm very proud of it this time. I think it's probably the most technically accomplished of the three films.

McKernan: They got the bugs worked out of the Zoptic system?

Reeve: No, we fired the Zoptic people. They were a drag. Zoptics does not work. It's trying to make flying in the camera instead of with the person. Dick Lester agreed with me wholeheartedly, is that you put the camera down and the people do their thing. That's the basics of comedy. If you go back to Keaton and Chaplin and all those guys, the camera is still and the people are running around. And this should extend to special effects as well. You can't do the tricks in the camera with human beings; they must be allowed as much freedom as possible.

So we have shots in this movie where I actually fly over real city traffic about four feet above the deck. Long, long flying shots over wheat fields that are all real outdoor stuff. There's a higher level—it's more ambitious and yet I feel the flying has gotten to the point where it's so good you don't even notice it, which is the ultimate compliment. People will sit there and take it for granted: "Oh yeah, he flies, of course."

It's a throwaway, if you know what I mean. We're not putting brackets around it.

McKernan: Undue emphasis on it.

Reeve: We're not calling attention to it, where the whole ad campaign for part one was "You'll Believe a Man Can Fly!"

McKernan: I always thought that was a big mistake.

Reeve: Big mistake.

McKernan: We already know he can fly.

Reeve: Yeah.

McKernan: Don't call attention to it.

Reeve: What we were trying to do in part one is say, "Look guys, this is not a joke, this is a real movie." But we know that now. But however the technical accomplishment of the flying is something that I'm proud of on this film. I have not seen it, but I think it's going to be pretty good.

McKernan: Getting back just a second here, I see I've got another note about the whole computer thing. I sort of see—or tell me if I'm reading too much into this—sort of an antitechnological bias in a lot of movies—

Reeve: Umm-hmm.

McKernan: —and I think of Luthor's use of technology and rockets in the first film, his black box in the second film, and the molecule chamber that almost does Superman in, but of course saves him too, is there sort of an antitechnological bias now with the ultimate computer [*in Superman III*]?

Reeve: There certainly is from Dick Lester's point of view, and he in fact got this idea from a discussion that I had with him about another script, totally non-related. It had to do with computers siphoning off when they round decimals on paychecks to the nearest number. There's a great mnay fractions of money, fractions of cents, that get stored away someplace, and the man who could tap on into that would have a windfall. That's one of the premises of the movie is that as we move into the future and toward high-tech we must try not to move away from *people*. And that's Lester's bias and my bias and it very definitely works into the story. The computer ends up being the thing that steals your humanity, that keeps us from relating to each other.

McKernan: In other words, we have to make sure that we run the computer and not vice-versa.

Reeve: Yeah. And to see that getting a machine to do all our work for us is not necessarily a good idea.

McKernan: Could Superman become cynical with all the Lex Luthors and Ross Websters trying to do him in?

Reeve: I don't know. See, that gets too close to making him a real person. I don't know, you simply don't have a film without a villain of some kind. So I've taken so much for granted I've never asked myself that question.

McKernan: I'm really getting into it here.

Reeve: That's fine, but you see I don't—when I play him, on the set and doing the work, then I really try to step inside and it's like Superman— like any real hero—doesn't judge people that much. He does what he needs to be done in his view but he doesn't ever lecture or at least he tries not to lecture. He doesn't tell people you shouldn't live this way, you're bad, you're wrong. See, I've tried to get away from that sort of moralizing, self-righteous side of Superman. He simply calls the shots as he sees them and helps where he's needed while trying to keep a low profile. But then when I leave it I never, and sit down and—I mean, Christ, the questions that people have come up with about the symbolism of it are really quite frightening. Religious figures who call up and ask if I'm aware of the responsibilities of being a contemporary Christ figure and things like that. And hey Jack, I'm an actor from New Jersey. I can't be responsible for that.

So what it comes down to, you're asking a question that I've never addressed. You see what I mean?

McKernan: Yes.

Reeve: Okay.

McKernan: How do you think *Superman III* will do against the other big summer movies, *Return of the Jedi* and the two James Bonds [*Octopussy* and *Never Say Never Again*]?

Reeve: I don't know, that's all marketing stuff. I just make the films and try to make a work that everyone's proud of. What happens to it at the box office or reviews or something I don't know because I'm, you know, you can't carry the weight around. You have to do it and then let yourself go, do you know what I mean?

McKernan: Yeah.

Reeve: It's like sailing a boat and constantly looking at the wake. You have to look at the waves ahead of you. You've got to look at the clouds and the wind in front of you, and not where you've just been.

McKernan: Did you need any special training for the role this time around?

Reeve: No, just review. Just I fell right back into it without any problems. The first week I felt awkward, I felt slight resistance to training again, particularly since the other work that I've done in the last couple of years has always required a thin body—*Deathtrap*, *Monsignor*, *Fifth of July*. I've been down to 185-190 and to go back to 220 was not a lot of fun. But I've done it.

McKernan: What's next on the horizon for Christopher Reeve?

Reeve: I think my next project at the moment I'm planning to do a film with Carl Reiner called *Lost in August*, which is a comedy about people in analysis in New York and what happens when *all* the shrinks go on vacation at the same time. As they *do*, they all go out of town in August and come back Labor Day. And having created a dependency in these people and then leave them stranded. That's probably on for May/June, that area. And then I'm thinking about doing a film called *The Aviator*, which I'll probably do in Yugoslavia in August/September.

McKernan: This is another wacky question, but I'll get right to it, Do you ever think it's strange coincidence that the actor who played Superman on television—George Reeves—had a name that was so similar to yours?

Reeve: You see, I don't have that name. He's Reeves, I'm Reeve, and it's a *big* difference. It's like the difference between Johnson and Johnston.

McKernan: Yeah, I know, I realize that. I cringed at the Special Olympics [*Superman II*] Premiere last year when Eunis Kennedy Shriver put the extra "S" in announcing your name.

Reeve: "And now a word from Chris Reeves," yeah.

McKernan: I gritted my teeth, like *"No!"*

Reeve: I always tell people that I took the "S" off Reeves and put it on my chest.

McKernan: You're resigned yourself very good-naturedly to a really stupid question.

Reeve: You know, there's certain things you just cannot—I don't know, to use a sort of a California hot-tub phrase, you can't let yourself be the *effect* of all those things. That's "external noise," you know what I mean?

McKernan: Yeah.

Reeve: And if I were to be that way that would mean that every time something stupid happened in a gossip column I'd get upset. For some reason they were convinced, the gossip people were convinced that Gaye [Exton] and I were having another child. And they had her pregnant for a good 19 months before they figured out that there was no baby. And never had been planned or anything. Our son Matthew is three. But I used to be the effect of all that stuff, go take the rides up and down with these sort of changes in fortune or perception. That is all external noise. You just let it go. So, that's what I do with all that.

McKernan: Yeah, I've been collecting interviews—

Reeve: You know where there's a good one—

McKernan: There's a good one in *Cosmopolitan*.

Reeve: Yeah, that's one of the best.

McKernan: I thought that was really good. [The article referred to here is titled "Christopher Reeve: A Surprising, Super Man," published in the March 1983 issue of *Cosmopolitan* magazine.]

Reeve: Finally, this lady Joan Barthel, who's a very accomplished novelist, actually, she came along because they had sent another girl who was just so...and stuff that I just really jumped on her. And in fact she writes about it in this article, says about this girl, and I reduced her to tears. But this lady had been asking me about my childhood, and I was talking about it, she said, "Oh well that's not interesting, I want the funny anecdotes."

I said "Look lady, if I tell you my life, and I tell you meaningful things that I think the audience will relate to, and you tell me that's not funny enough I want you to get right out of this room."

But then Joan Barthel came along, and the basic thing is she just let me be. And as a result she let me sort of reveal. You learn more about who I am by just letting me talk for two days and the trip to the mountains and stuff, than if you have a slant on the story.

I know you guys are coming from a science-fiction angle, and a tech angle, and a future angle, which is all fine, but you're not digging in for personal stuff. But Jesus, when these people get going and they've got some assignment from their editor that they've gotta come up with this angle on Superman it inevitably leads to a crunch. In terms of that, if they could all be like that [Joan Barthel's *Cosmopolitan* article] that would be wonderful. This lady was great. So that is, I stand by every word in that article.

McKernan: That was really good. I have another one here from a recent Sunday newspaper supplement magazine —

Reeve: That's a bad one.

McKernan: She was horrible.

Reeve: She just didn't like me because I wasn't pushing her buttons.

McKernan: Yeah.

Reeve: She really wanted to be stroked, too.

McKernan: She should walk the plank at your next cruise.

Reeve: Yeah, well I keep a list. She won't be invited back on the next cruise.

McKernan: Is there anything you'd want to say to our readers? You know, we're a sort of a science-fiction/tech type bunch. Do you enjoy science fiction at all?

Reeve: I hate to tell you this, but I'm not a science-fiction buff.

McKernan: That's okay, I'm not either.

Reeve: I tend to read biographies mostly. Or things that I need to know to learn things, like books on navigation or stuff like that. No, nothing more than "Hello, I hope they enjoy the film."

McKernan: I'll let you go, I really appreciate you taking the time, I can't tell you how much I appreciate it.

Reeve: You're welcome. I hope this third one makes it because there's some very good stuff in there and you know I would tell you more but I haven't seen it so I want to see how it comes out.

McKernan: Here's the last inevitable question: Do you think you'll do a number four?

Reeve: No, I guarantee you I won't. Because I don't want these films to become like a series, where they become formula stuff. And I think each of the three films has its own life, stands on its own two feet, and each has interesting new material. But you should quit while you're ahead, you know? And it has nothing to do with my life or casting or any of that kind of stuff. It's just simply I—money can't buy satisfaction and I've gotta do stuff that I'm happy with. They've gone on to *Supergirl* and we've had long talks and about "How much money would it take to get you to do *Superman IV*?" and I said "Don't bother, you know? Don't bother." It just isn't—you've got to move in your life and you're not, you know, we all had a good time in senior year in high school, but you can't stay there. So, not that I'm equating Superman with the senior year in high school, but the idea that you mustn't get stuck on any one thing in your life.

McKernan: Okay, thanks very much, Chris.

Reeve: Right, so long.

Chapter Four

"Your Attention Please!"

As the 1940s dawned, television was still a distant dream and radio was king, entertaining and informing millions of Americans daily with programs to suit practically every audience. Among the largest of these were kids listening to radio serial adventures of their favorite newspaper strip, comic book, and movie serial heroes. These broadcasts featured histrionic announcers, convincing sound effects, and dramatic organ interludes, all of which combined to paint vivid pictures of action and suspense in the theaters of young minds. Characters such as Little Orphan Annie, Flash Gordon, and Dick Tracy not only had thrilling 15-minute daily continuing adventures, they also helped sell millions of dollars of Ovaltine, Popsicles, Quaker Oats, and other products consumed by youngsters.

After hitting the jackpot with Superman's 1938 debut in *Action Comics* No. 1, which set records for newsstand comic-book sales, National (DC) Comics' live-wire owners Harry Donenfeld and Jack Liebowitz immediately sought to diversify Superman's media exposure as the owners of other youth-oriented characters had done. National's first "trans-media" Superman venture was with the McClure syndicate, which premiered a daily newspaper strip featuring the hero on January 16, 1939. A separate full-color Sunday page was added on November 5, 1939. Like Superman comic books, both were enthusiastically received by a nationwide audience.

Next came radio. Donenfeld and Liebowitz hired writer Robert Maxwell to develop a Superman radio serial, and after shopping around a few pilot episodes to radio stations and sponsors, the first official episode of *The Adventures of Superman* debuted on February 12, 1940 as a 15-minute thrice-weekly transcription service sold to individual stations. Each installment included a "cliffhanger" ending, typical of radio and movie serials. Recordings still exist of that first episode, which includes an early version of the Superman litany so familiar to us now:

"Boys and girls, your attention please! Presenting a new, exciting radio program featuring the amazing adventures of an amazing and incredible personality. Faster than an airplane! More powerful than a locomotive! Impervious to bullets! Up in the sky! Look! It's a giant bird, It's a plane! It's [hurricane wind sound effect begins] Superman!"

"And now Superman. A being no larger than an ordinary man, but possessed of powers and abilities never before realized on earth. Able to leap into the air an eighth of a mile at a single bound. Hurdle a 20-story building with ease. Race a high-powered bullet to its target. Lift tremendous weights and bend solid steel in his bare hands as if it were paper."

The radio Superman was an instant success, and it soon spread to ten Mutual network stations. Three months later the show's audience rating was the highest of any juvenile radio serial. By mid-1942 Superman's 15-minute episodes were broadcast live Monday through Friday over the entire Mutual network. Superman comics, meanwhile, were selling in excess of one million copies per issue, and the McClure Syndicate's Superman newspaper strip was being published in 300 daily and 90 Sunday papers, with a readership of over 20 million. And since December 1941, the Max Fleischer animation studios in Miami were releasing a series of Technicolor Superman cartoon shorts that Paramount Pictures distributed to theaters nationwide for presentation prior to major motion pictures. Superman had truly become a "trans-media" superstar, outshining many of his rivals in just a few years.

Radio's Superman demonstrated even more dramatically than its print counterparts that National had something more on its hands than just another four-color character for young audiences. According to the April 29, 1946 issue of *Newsweek*, "40 percent of his [Superman's] audience… is grown up." A March 3, 1947 article in *The New Republic* listed weekly listenership of Superman at 4.5 million. Evidence of this radio show's popularity is seen in the 1943 Humphrey Bogart movie *All Through the Night*, which includes a character likening strange events in his Nazi-infiltrated Manhattan neighborhood to the nightly mysteries on the Superman radio program. Rather impressive for character introduced only five years earlier.

The radio actor that portrayed Superman was Clayton "Bud" Collyer, who later became familiar to television audiences as the host of *To Tell the Truth* (1956-1967). In an undated interview included on a 1984 Radiola Records LP of four chapters of the radio series, Collyer recalled winning the role of the first broadcast Superman:

"It was a funny thing on that show, because when we all came to audition for this new idea, this Superman thing, we all knew about the comic. They didn't know how it should be played, whether they wanted one man for each part—Clark Kent and Superman—or whether they wanted two.

"And when I heard that I was auditioning for it I fought with Bob Maxwell who owned the rights to the thing, and I said, 'This is not for me....'

"He said 'Well, just audition, and we'll use you in some parts when and if it goes on the air.'

"Well it *did* go on the air, and he said, 'You're Superman!' And I tried to walk out of the show. Then, of course, it grew into a magnificent career-within-a-career. It was great fun. It was a great way to get all your inhibitions out. Fantasy, if played honestly and whole-hog, is great."

In addition to Collyer, the regular radio cast of *The Adventures of Superman* radio cast usually consisted of Joan Alexander as Lois Lane,

Julian Noa as Perry White, Jackie Kelk (later replaced by Jack Grimes) as Jimmy Olsen, and Jackson Beck as the announcer. Beck would also occasionally pinch-hit as Jimmy Olsen's young sidekick Beany Martin, occasional villains, and even Alfred Pennyworth, Batman's English butler.

More than anyone else, however, it was Beck's deep, distinctive, authoritative voice that imbued the radio Superman with a sense of excitement and expectation right from the start of each episode: *"Faster than a speeding bullet!* [sound effect of machine-gun fire], *More powerful than a locomotive!* [sound effect of express train]," etc.

Beck continued his voice-over career right up until his death in 2004 at the age of 92, when his rich baritone could still be heard in commercials for Kellogg's, Thomson's Water Seal, and Little Caesar's pizza, among others—just as impressive in the era of digital technology as it was in the wax-recording radio days of the 1930's. I interviewed him in 1995, and the conversation began with his statement that producer Maxwell hired him as narrator in 1943 to replace the voice of series writer/director George Lowther (also the author of a 1942 *Adventures of Superman* novel).

"Lowther tried to do the whole thing by himself and it finally wore him down," Beck remembered. "He had several shows to do, so he couldn't really pay attention. So he quit Superman and I came on as narrator. He directed for a while, and then he left that to do the show next door. Then Allen Ducovny came on to direct.

"I'd done a lot of things before I got around to doing Superman," Beck continued, recalling that the series originated from the Mutual Broadcasting/WOR Studios at 1440 Broadway, in Manhattan. "But I was pleased and excited by having been chosen to do it. Maxwell I knew very well; he had a production company and I actually worked for him. I'd finish one show, go out the door, take ten steps, and be inside the next door's studio and do another show. You took these things as a matter of course. It's just like going to work in a factory; you knew what you're going to do, and you knew what the characters are going to do. And so you go in and you knock 'em off."

Beck added that Maxwell's wife, Jessica, also directed the series, working with her husband, Ducovny, and others in an independent production company under contract to National.

The Adventures of Superman radio series was not a repetition of stories published in comic books and newspaper strips, but a hotbed of creativity that would originate such permanent Superman elements as Jimmy Olsen, Kryptonite, and X-ray vision. Such innovations were needed to meet the challenges of coming up with consistent and novel stories for an all-powerful character occupying large quantities of airtime every week. One continuity had Superman slumped at the bottom of a rowboat for two weeks, stunned from the effects of kryptonite and only able to grunt. Others had Batman guest-starring. The real objective of these storylines, however, was to give Collyer time for a much-needed vacation. Live broadcasting became the rule for the show, as it eliminated the need to make duplicate transcription discs for every station. The cast was a well-oiled machine that rarely made mistakes. But writing the show could be a challenge.

"The hardest thing about writing the scripts was 'What can you do for suspense to have a cliffhanger at the end of every 15-minute daily episode?'" recalled former Superman radio scriptwriter Ed Langley, whom I interviewed in 1985, "A railroad train runs across his chest; it doesn't hurt him, it hurts the train! Where do you get the suspense from?"

"I was a young writer in my twenties, and an older writer in his fifties said 'I've got it! The one thing Superman can't do is strike a match on a cake of soap!' And that was a kind of 'peg' that we used to explore what he couldn't do."

Langley recalls there being as many as seven alternating writers on the show at any one time, with each assigned to do a story that would run in ten installments over the course of two weeks. A struggling actor in 1940, Langley connected with the Superman radio series through Collyer, who was a family friend, and was hired by Lowther.

Langley also wrote for radio star Fred Allen's *Allen's Alley*, and he once penned a seven-minute BBC-style parody of *The Adventures of Superman* for it.

"We slowed it all down," Langley said, "and Fred Allen, doing a British accent, says, 'Hey, chap, look up at that fog. I think it's a Hurricane or a Spitfire...no, I think it's that chap based on the philosophy of Friedrich Nietzsche called Superman. He's quite capable of shoving the Thames up some minor estuary....'"

Perhaps the most notable aspect of the radio Superman, however, was its exploration of issues relating to ethnic and religious tolerance. Such scripts predominated after World War II, and were fairly remarkable for a 1940s radio show aimed ostensibly at young people. Of course, as the previously mentioned *Newsweek* article indicates, *The Adventures of Superman* also had a sizable adult audience.

"*Superman* is the first children's program to develop a social consciousness," *Newsweek* reported in 1946. "To do it, Superman Inc., the company that controls the Man of Tomorrow in all his media, had to sell the idea to the Kellogg [sic] Co. sponsors and Mutual—two perpetual worriers over the response of Southern and reactionary listeners. Currently Robert Maxwell, radio director of Superman Inc., feels he has won a strong point. 'Tolerance is rampant in Battle Creek,' he says. 'Every bit of Pep in Rice Krispies is tolerant.'"

"The first sequence involves Superman with a tough bunch of young intolerants who gang up on an effort to establish an Inter-Faith Community House. For moral assistance, Superman is supplied with a Catholic priest of the Crosby-Father O'Malley type and a young Jewish rabbi, a former lightweight boxer at his seminary."

The previously cited March 3, 1947 *New Republic* article quoted an executive at Kenyon and Eckhardt, Kellogg's ad agency:

"All the parents' organizations are congratulating us on the show. The psychologists tell us we're planting a 'thought egg' in the kids' minds. Anyway, the wonderful thing is that our Hooper's [radio ratings of the 1940's] have actually gone up since the campaign started...this tolerance theme is good business."

"Nothing went on the air without having first passed through the Child Study Association," Beck recalled. "And we took on things that hadn't really been touched, especially in juvenile radio."

Beck added an interesting anecdote to our conversation that has perplexed many fans of the radio and television versions of *The Adventures of Superman* ever since he first related it. Some even claim that "it can't possibly be true" because of a lack of documentation, but I'll present it again here nevertheless.

A New York-based actor, Beck claimed he had a chance meeting in June 1951 with another actor living in Manhattan at the time who would also soon be employed by Superman, Inc.—George Reeves, today remembered as the star of *The Adventures of Superman* television series. Ironically, their meeting had nothing to do with either man's involvement with the character.

"I'll tell you a story about him," Beck confided. "I only met him once. I was best man at his wedding, and I never even knew the guy," Beck said of Reeves.

"A friend of mine roomed with Reeves. He called me up and said, 'Jack, what are you doing Sunday afternoon?' I checked with my wife, and said 'Nothing. What's up?'"

"And he said, 'A friend of mine, my roommate, as a matter of fact, is getting married and we need a best man.'"

"'What's wrong with you?' I asked."

"'Well, I—for various reasons—can't do it,' he replied."

"So I said 'All right.'"

"And he said, 'Would your wife be matron of honor?'"

"And I said, 'Sure, I guess so.' So he gave me the address, a place on Gramercy Park, in Manhattan, and told us what time to be there."

"So we get there that Sunday, I brought a bottle of champagne, and we walked up five flights of stairs to this apartment on the top floor. It's absolutely empty except for a couple of sleeping bags, a couple of wooden chairs, and a table—a typical starving actor's home. So I'm introduced to Mr. Reeves and the blushing bride. He was due to leave for the coast the following day to do the picture [*Superman and the Mole Men*], and so I said 'It's nice to meet you,' and so on and so forth. And that's just about where the conversation began and ended."

"Finally a minister arrived. I don't know who he was or where they got him. He looked like a parody of what you'd think of as an old-time preacher. He was a thin, grey man with a black suit, and a hat, and a white shirt, and a black tie. He was more like an undertaker than anything else. And he had a Bible in his hand, and we were introduced to him. And then the ceremony took place."

"I signed all the papers, I had to sign the license, the witness, and all of that. And then I said, 'Well, I brought the champagne, do you have four —or five—glasses?'"

"And they scurried around and finally found a couple of glasses and a couple of cups. So we all drank to the newlyweds, and my wife and I left. The next day he flew to California to do Superman. And that's the first and last time I ever saw George Reeves."

Beck insisted that the story is true. Its time frame would place it after Reeves' 1950 divorce from actress Ellanora Needles and before his relationship with Toni Mannix, wife of MGM president Eddie Mannix (if you've seen the 2006 movie *Hollywoodland*, I need not explain further). As of today, however, no official records have surfaced to confirm that this mystery wedding took place.

Nevertheless, George Reeves traveled to Hollywood that week to begin filming the theatrical *Mole Men* pilot and first season of the television episodes of *The Adventures of Superman*. He was not alone on that journey. Also along for the ride was Maxwell, who would co-produce the series in partnership with Bernard Luber, and National editorial director Whitney Ellsworth, visiting to keep his eye on filming for his New York bosses. They were, in fact, part of an even larger east-to-west exodus of creative talent from the New York-based radio industry, and that was because of television. No longer the distant dream mentioned at the beginning of this chapter, by 1951 television was 'the next big thing.' Buoyed by post-war scientific advances that had solved the medium's early technical hurdles and by new federal standards for telecasting, new television stations were sprouting up like weeds from coast to coast. The number of U.S. consumer television sets rose from 6,000 in 1946 to 12 million by 1951. Four years later half of all U.S. homes would have a "TV set." A new California "gold rush" was underway to fill television broadcast schedules with content, especially for the vast new postwar "baby boom" audience.

Other radio series transitioning to television included *The Lone Ranger*, *Dick Tracy*, *Captain Midnight*, *Dragnet*, and *Gunsmoke*, just to name a few. It was a major change for producers. Where once four actors standing around a microphone with a sound-effects technician sufficed to bring a story to life, producers were now faced with the challenge of actually filming a half-hour motion picture depicting all the things formerly conveyed solely by audio. In the case of Superman, the titular character now had to be visually depicted bending steel in his bare hands and leaping tall buildings in a single bound. This required an order of magnitude upgrade in the cost of producing every show, especially the effects-laden *Adventures of Superman*.

Fortunately for this character, two live-action Superman movie serials had been produced by Columbia Pictures, in 1948 and 1950, which provided a "proof of concept" that the challenge of translating radio's Superman to film could be done. Actor Kirk Alyn portrayed Superman in the serials, the most profitable ever produced. *Superman and the Mole Men,* a theatrical feature starring George Reeves was released in November 1951 and served as a pilot for the television series, which began airing in Chicago in late 1952.

The end of the *Adventures of Superman* radio series wasn't, however, the end of its cast's association with the Man of Steel. Sixteen years later, Beck, Joan Alexander, Jack Grimes, and Julian Noa all worked with actor Bob Holiday, star of the 1966 Hal Prince Broadway musical *"It's a Bird...It's a Plane...It's Superman,"* to record *The Official Adventures of Superman*, an LP record of four Superman comic book adventures. Later that year the cast reunited with Bud Collyer to reprise their radio roles as the voices featured on *The New Adventures of Superman*, the character's first-ever made-for-television Saturday-morning cartoon series. Also in the credits were Superman radio producer Allen Ducovny.

"They wanted as many of the 'original' voices as they could get, and I was one of them," Beck says. "I went in there and did a couple of parts, and the narration."

From small-screen Saturday-morning television cartoons to big-screen live-action movie epics, Superman continued to conquer new frontiers with the 1978 release of *Superman: The Movie* starring Christopher Reeve. This film and its three sequels started a new genre of filmmaking —the superhero blockbuster—which continues to dominate the box office today.

That said, radio-style Superman audio adventures never totally disappeared. A handful of vintage Superman radio series episodes were issued on LP records by small labels starting in the 1960's. During the 1970's Peter Pan Records released a series of youth-oriented book-and-record sets and separate LP records of original Superman audio adventures reminiscent of the radio show. In 1989 Shan-Lon Enterprises/ MPI Inc. produced *The Man of Steel* series, a six-part audiocassette version of the DC Comics' revamping of the Superman legend. And just one year before, to coincide with Superman's fiftieth birthday, the BBC elaborately revived Superman's radio career with the first of three digitally recorded new radio productions. Originally airing on BBC Radio 4 on June 5, 1988, *Superman on Trial*, written by Dirk Maggs, featured Stuart Milligan as Superman, Shelley Thompson as Lois Lane, and Vincent Marzello as Jimmy Olsen. These were followed-up by *The Adventures of Superman* (1990) and *Doomsday and Beyond* (1993).

This newfound love for Superman on radio may have been the impetus for a remarkable development for fans of the original series. In 1997 The Smithsonian Institution Press in association with Radio Spirits began releasing a series of boxed sets of original 1940's Superman radio serial continuities digitally remastered by expert audio archivist Fred Shay. Using original transcription discs that had been stored in a Brooklyn warehouse for more than 50 years, Shay utilized a vintage radio station turntable and coated each record with a dishwashing liquid mixture to reduce surface hiss and obtain high-quality audio restorations (see Chapter Fourteen).

Each Smithsonian/Radio Spirits set included a booklet written by noted old-time radio expert Anthony Tollin that provided historical context, rare photographs, original airdates, and cast lists. Radio Spirits released a total of seven such volumes on both tape cassette and CD. The company's timing was excellent. Audio books had already become popular with the introduction of the Sony Walkman portable cassette tape player during the 1980's. A CD Walkman was introduced in 1999. A new generation of audio-content consumers used these products to discover the fun of old-time radio. The growth of the Internet furthered the popularity of this trend into the 2000's, and content providers responded with such titles as: *Kingdom Come*, based on the four-issue comic book

Radio artifacts were part of the 1988 *Superman: Many Lives, Many Worlds* exhibit at the Smithsonian National Museum of American History.

miniseries and subsequent novel by Elliot S. Maggin; *Superman Lives!*, a 2005 Time Warner Audiobooks reissue of the BBC's 1993 *Doomsday and Beyond*, which begins with a re-creation of the classic Superman radio "Faster than a speeding bullet" introduction; an audio dramatization of the Tom De Haven novel *It's Superman* (2005); a novelization of the *Superman Returns* movie (2006); and many other selections.

Today's *Superman & Lois* television series owes much to the wizardry of modern digital visual effects, but the audience for the original *Adventures of Superman* radio series knew all about amazing imagery. As the old saying goes, *"I prefer radio to TV because the pictures are better."*

Chapter Five

The Golden Anniversary of the Man of Steel

In 1988 Superman was 50 years old, or at least that was how many years it was since his first appearance in *Action Comics*. February 29th is Superman's birthday. I *know*. I attended his fiftieth birthday party at the Puck Building in New York City. The date of that event, however, was February 26, 1988. Jenette Kahn, then-president/publisher of DC Comics, explained that that date was chosen because it was a Friday, which is not a school night. "We've waited a long time for this event," she added. "And while for us mere mortals, reaching our fiftieth year can be a shock, it is truly wonderful to know that Superman will go on and on."

Now, before you tell me that Superman's birthday is definitely *not* February 29th but instead some other date clearly specified in an important comic book story or television episode, please note that the idea initially began as a lark. DC editors explained tongue-in-cheek in comic book letter-to-the-editor columns that Superman remained "eternally youthful" because he was born on Leap Day, February 29, which occurs only once every four years. That math actually doesn't quite make sense; by this logic Superman would have been only 12 in 1988. Nevertheless, there was even a Time magazine cover story (published March 14, 1988) commemorating Superman's 50th birthday that declared the character's birth date as February 29.

No matter what date you claim, however, let's all agree that we're glad that Jerry Siegel and Joe Shuster invented Superman in the first place.

And we're grateful that so many talented people have contributed to creating his stories since 1938.

One of the great things about having been a Manhattan-based magazine editor was the opportunity to attend the occasional special event in the center of the media universe. I was editor of *Videography* at the time, a teleproduction trade magazine, and was delighted to receive an advance invitation to this party. DC Comics actually held four consecutive fiftieth birthday parties for Superman on the evening of February 26, 1988. Each was 70 minutes long (at 4:30, 6, 7:30, and 9pm) and the location was Manhattan's historic Puck Building. It was an appropriate venue, having been the home of *Puck* magazine from 1876 to 1918. *Puck* was a weekly publication of political cartoons and the ancestor of the modern comic book. The building's large galleries were well suited to containing the sold-out Superman birthday party crowds.

Tickets to each party cost $12 for adults and $6 for children (age 12 and under). For each ticket sold, DC Comics donated $1.00 to the National Foster Parent Association. ("Superman," Kahn noted during the proceedings, "is the world's most famous foster child.") Souvenir and licensed commemorative items were also sold at the party, with net proceeds donated to the NFPA. In addition to Kahn, DC Comics notables attending included editor emeritus Julius "Julie" Schwartz, artist Curt Swan, future DC president/publisher Paul Levitz, and New York City's then-mayor Edward Koch. Master event producer Robert F. Jani organized this "multimedia celebration." Ironically, none of the three surviving Superman actors at that time (the serials' Kirk Alyn, Broadway's Bob Holiday, or the movies' Chris Reeve) were there in person, but Superman was nevertheless present, projected onto large video screens in the form of excerpts from the Fleischer Studios Superman cartoons, the serials, *The Adventures of Superman* television series, and the Chris Reeve movies. Dozens of small children that had accompanied their parents sat on the floor at the far end of the room, gazing up at the screens, transfixed by scenes of Superman in action.

Each attendee received a Superman Birthday party coupon book good for Superman peanuts, Superman pretzels, an Armour hot dog, an Orangina soft drink, a Hostess Twinkie snack cake, and a Polaroid photo with a Superman or Lois Lane cutout figure. Each Hostess Twinkie snack cake was packaged in its own small box. Five thousand of these were stacked, brick-like, to build what resembled a giant Superman birthday cake. Also free to guests were special edition copies of the New York *Daily News*, which proclaimed Superman's birthday on the front cover. Elsewhere, a piece of Kryptonite, the Bottled City of Kandor (disappointingly, a cheap sandcastle candle in an empty plastic water jug), and a bent crowbar were displayed on pedestals as Superman artifacts. CNN reporter Jeanie Moss was on hand with her videographer and she filed a report that aired that night. I'm even in it for a brief second, wearing a suit and opening

DC Comics president Jenette Kahn and New York City mayor Edward Koch address the performers at Superman's fiftieth birthday party on February 26, 1988, in New York City.

my shirt to reveal a Superman T-shirt my wife had given me as a joke after one too many people told me I "look just like Clark Kent."

The party was but one event in Superman's year-long 1988 50th anniversary celebration, which also included an exhibit at Washington's Smithsonian National Museum of American History and a CBS one-hour Superman retrospective (*Superman's 50th Anniversary: A Celebration of the Man of Steel*) broadcast on February 29, 1988 (see Chapter Six).

Onstage at the February 26, 1988 party, a "Superman Celebration" musical revue featured Broadway-style singing and dancing by a group calling itself The Entertainment Company and young dancers known as Kids 2 Go. No Superman-specific songs were performed; instead The Entertainment Company sang a medley of the Pointer Sisters' "I'm So Excited," Kool & the Gang's "Celebration," and similar fare. Kids 2 Go then took the stage with an a cappella rendition of the John Williams theme, followed by a group chant:

"It's Superman!
Being fans of Superman is what we're all about!
He fights for peace and justice; he knows that truth wins out!
He's our superhero; he's what we want to be!
I always feel like Superman is right inside of me!
We gotta listen to his message; let's cheer throughout the land!
Wish him Happy Birthday! We love you Su-per-man!"

The Kids 2 Go youngsters then danced 1988-era hip-hop to several spirited numbers, displaying remarkable talent despite their tender years.

As their performance concluded I mingled in the crowd and spied Julie Schwartz, who I had met three years earlier when I visited DC Comics to pitch them on a Superman Fiftieth anniversary book. DC passed on my proposal but I spent an enjoyable half-hour with Julie as he showed me his First Fandom scrapbook from the early days (mid-1930's) of modern science fiction. I greeted Julie and took my little Sony tape recorder from my pocket. Here's a transcript of the interview.

McKernan: How far back does your career with Superman go?

Schwartz: Well actually two days ago I started my 45th year with DC Comics. But I took over the editing of Superman in 1971 until last year. I guess that's about 17 years of editing Superman. When I took over Superman I did a lot of things that were done by John Byrne; revitalizing Superman, decreasing his strength, making him more lovable, and so on.

McKernan: You made him a television reporter.

Schwartz: Yeah, but that didn't work out, did it? Very few people know that when Mario Puzo did the screenplay of the first Superman movie — and he came up to the office, did a lot of research, and talked to me — the first screenplay of the movie had Clark Kent as a television reporter.

McKernan: Really?

Schwartz: What happened is they decided to do sort of a "man on the street" interview and they went around asking people "Who is Clark Kent?" And everyone said "He's a reporter for the *Daily Planet*." And so they said "I think we made a mistake," and they re-wrote the script, taking him out of the television, and putting him back as a reporter.

McKernan: What do you think has made Superman last for 50 years?

Schwartz: Well, we all identify with Superman. We all identify with Clark Kent and secretly hope we someday could be Superman and do those heroic things that he does. We can lash out at our tormentors and get even with our schoolteachers and all the bullies that kick sand in our face. You know, Superman was the original double-identity theme as far as comics, but was of course borrowed from other sources — Zorro, the Scarlet Pimpernel, and so on.

McKernan: Do you think Superman will be around 50 years from now?

Schwartz: Well, he'll be around, I'll try to be around. Fair enough. I think he will. Many people say there are three fictional characters who are known worldwide. One is Superman, one is Sherlock Holmes, and one is Tarzan. No matter where you go in the world they all know these three people. So Superman is that popular, he's going to hang around.

McKernan: It must make you feel very proud to have worked on a character like that.

Schwartz: Sure does. And people come over to me out of nowhere, pass me on the street and say, "Can I have your autograph?" It makes me feel good.

[Julie Schwartz passed away on Febuary 8, 2004 at the age of 88.]

Our attention was then diverted back to the stage as Jenette Kahn introduced Mayor Edward Koch, who told the crowd:

"To be celebrating Superman's birthday together is very special. How old is he?"

"Fifty!" responded the Kids 2 Go youngsters.

"But how old does he look?" Koch added.

"Twenty!" agreed the audience.

"Superman is like Peter Pan; he never grows old," Koch continued. "And he's always there to protect the citizens of Metropolis. There is no crime that goes unpunished in Metropolis. Would that there were a Superman that *I* could have here in *this* city to protect *us* from crime. Wouldn't *that* be nice?"

After the cheering subsided, Koch concluded: "So let's say to Superman, May you live to 120, Superman!"

Metropolis has always been a thinly veiled version of New York City. It felt great to be at the center of the Superman universe on such an important evening. And I still cherish my Polaroid photos with the Superman and Lois Lane cutouts they had set up there.

Chapter Six

Superman's 50th Anniversary: A Celebration of the Man of Steel

Look, up in the sky! It's a bird, it's a plane, it's the most famous fictional character in history: Superman! The creation of cartoonist Joe Shuster and writer Jerry Siegel, Superman this year [this article was originally published in 1988] celebrates a half-century of exploits in comic books, newspaper strips, radio, movie serials, television, Broadway, and feature films. This mass media exposure has made the character recognizable in practically every corner of the world, and in the U.S. clichés about X-ray vision, quick changes in phone booths, and leaping tall buildings in a single bound are an integral part of American pop culture.

With these facts firmly in mind, DC Comics, Inc., owner of the Superman character, called on Broadway Entertainment executive producer Lorne Michaels and producer Mary Salter to create an hour-long television special for CBS that would do justice to this enduring folk hero. Michaels and Salter had previously produced a Broadway Entertainment fiftieth anniversary tribute to Bugs Bunny and the Warner Brothers animation department. Warner Communications subsidiary DC Comics felt that Broadway Entertainment was the right choice for the Superman project as well.

"Doing the Superman show is a different challenge than the cartoon special was," Salter explains. "For Superman we've created a strange hybrid that relies on original clips for about half the show, and original comedy for the rest."

To achieve the proper balance of humor necessary to pay homage to this fantasy character, Broadway's Michaels and Salter turned to director Robert Boyd. Boyd's previous credits include the Cinemax video production *Canadian Conspiracy*, a tongue-in-cheek look at the influence of Canadians in the American entertainment industry.

"This project is the same kind of thing as *Canadian Conspiracy*," Boyd explains, "in that I'm sort of playing with people's heads. I'm creating a reality and then staying true to it all the way through, but in a comical way. The show looks at things everyone takes for granted, and then puts a twist on them. It's a mock documentary on what it's like to live in the same city as Superman."

In addition to comic-book panels, the show uses clips from four major genres of Superman films made from 1941 to 1987: the Fleischer/Famous Studios theatrical cartoons, the Kirk Alyn serials, the George Reeves television series, and the Christopher Reeve movies.

"We've also shot original material of celebrities and of character roles — people on the street stuff," says Boyd, "it's done on location in Los Angeles and in the New York area. We've got gangsters who tell what it's like to fight against him, we've got Superman's dry cleaner, and Hal Holbrook talks about his one-man show, *An Evening With Superman*.

"We used Betacam because it helped the reality by giving us a news documentary look, and allowed us to go back and forth to the clips without getting in the way. We tried for a look similar to the *Adventures of Superman* television series. We kept set design simple and used a lot of light, because the television series was always overlit," Boyd explains. "Broadway Video did all of our video transferring and support, and gave me ¾-inch dailies of our Betacam shoots for off-lining. We also used The Rig, their computerized animation stand, to shoot comic book panels."

"Betacam gave me control, and for this shoot I loved it," explains Robert Leacock, director of photography on the Superman fiftieth anniversary project. "I care for lighting because I'm a documentary cameraman, and

I worked with Betacam as if it were film. It gave me the freedom to light the situation and go shoot it. We rented Ikegami HL-95 cameras and Sony BVW-25 VCRs from Flying Tiger Communications, in New York.

"Flying Tiger also provided us with Colortran film-lighting equipment and the grip stuff necessary to control it (egg crates, flags, nets, Rosco shower curtain, and gels). We chose flat lighting for the character parts to match the television series, and we lit the famous people not quite as softly, but in more of a documentary style."

Unit manager Peter Schulberg handled location scouting chores for the production, and sought architecture and settings reminiscent of the 1950's Superman television series. Among his discoveries that appear in the show are a well-preserved Victorian house in the New York suburb of Yonkers, a trailer park in Hoboken NJ, and a vintage printing press on Manhattan's West Side. The eastern Long Island community of Sag Harbor served as small-town USA.

Original location video production was only part of the challenge faced by Broadway Entertainment for the Superman special. The other half involved incorporating the existing film versions of the character that have been made during the last half century. Two of the genres came easily to the producers, supplied by Warner Communications on one-inch tape: the 17 Fleischer/Famous Studios Technicolor Superman theatrical cartoons from the early 1940s and the recent quartet of Christopher Reeve movies.

Superman, a 1948 Columbia Pictures movie serial, was also supplied by Warner, but a second serial, *Atom Man Vs. Superman* (1950), proved more elusive. Neither DC nor Warner had a copy, and the only known print was a 35mm nitrate negative at the Library of Congress that hadn't been opened in decades and was feared to be disintegrating. Broadway Entertainment had a VHS copy from a collector that they used for off-lining, but it wasn't broadcast quality.

"We wanted to feature the two serials a lot in the show because many people had never seen them," Boyd explains. "*Atom Man* is particularly full of wonderful footage, and we were hinging sequences on it, but we weren't even sure we'd get a print of it." Fortunately, Kirk Alyn, the star of the Superman serials, owned a 16mm copy of the film, and it became available to Broadway following an agreement between the actor and Warner to release the picture on home video.

The remaining film version of the Man of Steel to be included in the anniversary special was the 104 episodes of *The Adventures of Superman* series produced for television from 1951 to 1957. In a great stroke of foresight, DC Comics originally filmed the latter 52 of these in color, a full decade before color television came into widespread use. Although 16mm syndication prints of nearly all the episodes are plentiful, Michaels, Salter, and Boyd opted for the uncut, superior picture quality of the original 35mm negatives for transfer to tape.

"We had a problem with determining the most cost-effective way to view, transfer, and use this original material," Salter recalls. "To put everything on one-inch tape would have been cost-prohibitive."

Broadway's solution was to have researcher Rocco Caruso view all 104 episodes, pick the scenes the producers wanted, and then have those transferred to tape. "Transfer of these images," explained associate producer Juli Pari, "turned out to be the biggest ordeal of all."

Pari and Caruso discovered that the color negatives were in pristine condition except for those portions that included optical special effects shots (dissolves and fades). Those parts were found to be hot-spliced into the negative, several generations removed from the rest of the film, grainy and severely faded. Many of the scenes that were chosen had opticals in them, requiring time-consuming color-correction. Transfer and color correction were done at The Tape House Editorial Company, in New York, on a Rank Cintel Mark IIIC, with an Amigo color corrector and Faroudja encoder. The colorist on the project was Vincent Cervone.

Soundtracks presented another problem. "Most of the stuff hadn't been looked at in years," Caruso explains. "All of it had separate 35mm optical soundtrack, but instead of being on the side of the film, some of it was in the center—a system that no longer exists. For those we pulled the sound off the 16mm syndication prints, although sometimes that was a problem because there would be a few frames missing, and we'd have to go back and sync it up again."

Original music and effects tracks from the television series were loaned to the production by Jim Hambrick, Superman memorabilia expert whose collection is valued in excess of one million dollars. Hal Willner, whose credits include music for *Saturday Night Live*, cataloged this and other original music for use in the show.

For director Robert Boyd, having access to a wealth of original material for the project was not without its problems. "We had some difficult decisions to make," he says, reflecting on the total 48 minutes he had to work with for the one-hour special. "Viewers are going to be fascinated with the clips, and there are things that we thought should be in there, and have tried to include at the expense of almost anything else."

Boyd's decision-making process was aided by Douglas Jines, editor of the project. "When I came on the job I felt we needed a rough edit system that would help Robert experiment and work out his creative ideas," Jines explains. "For technical reasons we're calling it *off-off-lining*, and it's basically a cost-effective type of thing. We used a straight-cuts Sony 440 editor, with a Sony VO-5800 ¾-inch machine for the feed and a VO-5850 for the record VCR. We just push our ins and outs, and the rough cut we come up with should be 95 percent there."

"Then we'll get into a more sophisticated off-line situation with a Convergence 195, where we can build a list and do an auto-assemble, and find out if it goes together as we expect it to. After that we take it up to the tenth floor of Broadway Video to one of their three one-inch on-line suites to conform the show just as a film editor would go to a conformer to conform his film. We'll transfer the five-inch floppy from the Convergence to an eight-inch disk for Broadway Video's Sony 5000, and then it will be just a matter of changing reels."

Broadway Video, sister division of Broadway Entertainment, will also figure prominently in another important element of the Superman fiftieth anniversary special—computer graphics. Both the beginning and ending of the show will utilize Broadway Video's extensive computer graphic and digital video effects equipment—appropriate considering Superman's humble origins as a 2D graphic on a comic-book page.

Jonathan Applebaum, special effects editor, describes the supergraphic treatment planned for the show: "We'll do 3D animation of the Superman S-shield for the beginning of the show using our Alias 3D system, which has a Celerity rendering engine. The ending of the show will be even more interesting, because it brings into play

VIDEOGRAPHY

FEBRUARY 1988/$3.00

PRODUCTION REPORT
PRODUCTION SWITCHER GUIDE
SAN FRANCISCO

different areas of both Broadway Video and traditional cel animation."

The ending will combine black-and-white serial footage of Superman flying with new cel animation—in color—showing him gliding over a modern skyline and landing in a comic-book page. A comic book cover then closes over him to end the program. The sequence will involve the use of a Quantel Paintbox, an Abekas A62, and a Quantel Mirage for the final page turn.

Although the serials were live-action films, they used cartoon animation to show Superman in flight. "We've loaded a flying sequence from the original serial into the Paintbox," Applebaum explains, "and Sharon Haskell, our Paintbox artist, traced Superman out of the scene, on paper with a special Paintbox stylus that has a ballpoint pen in it. We then gave those line drawings to a film animator, who'll match the old footage and continue Superman's flight. After that we'll load the new cels back into the Paintbox, colorize them, and create a matte for each cel so that we can key it in over new skyline footage." Applebaum adds that this final sequence will be intercut with new video of a crowd shouting the traditional lines: "It's a bird, it's a plane, it's Superman!"

Comic books launched Superman's career fifty years ago, but when the Broadway Entertainment special airs on the 29th of this month it will be video that sends him flying off for another half century of never-ending battles for truth, justice, and the American way.

Superman's 50th Anniversary: A Celebration of the Man of Steel was broadcast on the CBS television network at 8pm on Monday, February 29, 1988. It is included in the *Superman Ultimate Collector's Edition* DVD set and *The Superman Motion Picture Anthology 1978-2006* Blu-ray Disc set.

Chapter Seven

Look! Up on the Screen!

Superman's long movie and television career mirrors the evolution of visual effects technology. From the Technicolor Fleischer Studios cartoons, to the Columbia serials, to television's *Adventures of Superman*, to *Superman: The Movie*, to early uses of digital imaging in *Superboy* and *Lois & Clark*, to today's effects-heavy *Superman & Lois* series can be seen a continuum of progress in moving-image content creation.

Trick photography has been part of motion pictures since their very beginning. Early filmmakers such as the Lumière brothers, George Méliès, and Thomas Edison all understood the power of double exposures, jump cuts, and shooting through painted glass as ways to amaze audiences. Such tricks had been well established for half a century by the time Superman made his screen debut in a 1941 Fleischer Studios cartoon. Animation was also a mature craft, but the realistic artwork, feature-style direction, brilliant Technicolor photography, and dramatic musical score by composer Sammy Timberg all combined to powerfully convey the wonder of this new screen hero. Superman's first cartoon (one of a series of 17 theatrical shorts) narrowly missed winning an Academy Award to Mickey Mouse, but subsequent installments impressed audiences so vividly that depictions of quick changes in phone booths became an indelible Superman cliché even though it was seldom seen in comic books and never seen in his 1950's television series. Fast-forward 37 years, and director Richard Donner exploited the idea for a quick laugh in the dramatic helicopter rescue scene in *Superman: The Movie*.

In 1948 Superman starred in his first of two live-action serials, produced by Sam Katzman at Columbia Pictures. Movie serials had been a staple of the cinema since 1912, with many newspaper strip, comic book, and radio heroes providing the inspiration for these weekly matinee cliffhanger shorts. Superman, however, was a special challenge, requiring flying shots to rival what the Fleischers had done. Katzman's solution was to use Fleischer-style animation when the wires keeping actor Kirk Alyn aloft couldn't be concealed. Artist Howard Swift's hand-drawn animation on top of live-action background photography recalled Fleischer's fluid style; *Superman* and its 1950 sequel *Atom Man Vs. Superman* became the most successful serials of all time.

Superman and the Mole Men, a theatrical feature made the following year introduced actor George Reeves in the title role and served as a pilot for the forthcoming *Adventures of Superman* television series. Animation yielded to wire- and springboard-assisted takeoffs and traditional process-photography of Reeves filmed "flying" against sky backgrounds. The first filmed television series featuring motion-picture style optical effects, the *Adventures of Superman*'s 104 episodes (the latter 52 shot in color a decade before color telecasts became the norm) quickly became the most successful syndicated series on television for many years.

Two decades after the cameras stopped rolling on Superman's adventures on the small screen, film producers Alexander and Ilya Salkind began work on their historic, big-screen mega-budget movie version. Motion picture visual effects really hadn't advanced all that much in the intervening 20 years, so the expert British special-effects technicians assigned to the task were nearly driven to distraction over the course of many months trying to make audiences believe actor Christopher Reeve could fly. Superman's big-screen flying would be far more elaborate than anything done previously for television, so the movie's effects wizards had to push the boundaries of analog filmmaking as far as they could go in what was still (as of 1978) the pre-digital age. Solutions included painting-out wires, traveling matte photography, rotoscoping, and an early computer-controlled lensing technology known as Zoptics, after its creator Zoran Perisic. He and five of his *Superman: The Movie* colleagues won Special Achievement Visual Effects Oscars for their work on the film. Three sequels and a *Supergirl* feature followed before the Salkinds returned planet Krypton's Kal-El to the small screen for his next series of adventures.

The Boy of Steel

A half-hour *Adventures of Superboy* television series pilot film had been made for television in 1961 by *Adventures of Superman* producer Whitney Ellsworth, but failed to sell. Fast-forward 26 years, and the Salkinds successfully launched a live-action *Superboy* series (later renamed *The Adventures of Superboy*), as a half-hour first-run syndicated television series in October 1988. The show told the background tales of the young Superman's years at the *Siegel* School of Journalism at *Shuster* College. The Salkinds leveraged the hard-won expertise that

Form-fitting body pan and blue-velvet backdrop used for studio flying shots in the Christopher Reeve Superman films and the *Superboy* television series.

their production crews had learned while making the highly successful Christopher Reeve Superman movies during the previous decade. They re-used such custom-built equipment as a body pan on the end of a counterbalanced steel beam for flying Superboy actors John Haymes Newton and Gerard Christopher in front of a massive blue-velvet backdrop, and a sophisticated cable-pulley harness originally created for Reeve's outdoor flying shots. (A green backdrop would have worked much better for Superboy's blue costume, but the Ultimatte Corp. hadn't perfected it yet. *Lois & Clark*, produced a few years later, *was* able to employ a green-screen color-difference system.)

Key to the Salkinds' new live-action *Superboy* series was their decision to film in Florida, as opposed to England where the Reeve movies had been made (except for location scenes). Their timing was perfect. In 1988 Orlando's Disney World opened Disney-MGM Studios, which was designed to serve as an actual working production facility and tourist attraction appealing to the public's fascination with moviemaking. The facility included fully equipped sound stages, craft services, and street-facade "back lots." Florida had attempted to compete with Hollywood as a center of motion-picture production as far back as the silent-movie days. Local business boosters had long promoted the state's year-round sunny weather, which is essential for film photography. Many features were produced in Florida over the years, including such classics as *Beneath the 12-Mile Reef* (1953), and television series such as *Flipper* were based there during the 1960s, but the 1988 opening of Disney-MGM and its nearby competitor, Universal Studios/Florida, put film and television production into high gear in the state. Its "right to work" laws also helped, reportedly freeing local producers from some of Hollywood's costly labor requirements.

"It's very agreeable; the weather, the crews," producer Ilya Salkind noted in 1988, adding that it's easier to shoot a television series that takes place in the U.SA. *in the U.S.A.* "Getting the real Americana, from shooting at the college, to the windows of the college, or the [American] cars; to do this on a constant basis in England would have been very difficult."

An even more important aspect of *Superboy*, however, was its pioneering use of early computer-based effects and editing systems to affordably achieve advanced visual wonders while deliverng a new episode on a tight schedule each week. Big-budget *Star Wars*, *Star Trek*, and *Indiana Jones* movies had spearheaded R&D into applying new advances in computer imaging into filmmaking applications. Movie audiences became accustomed to seeing impressive new effects and expected to see them on television as well. Increased audience appetites for visual sophistication prompted entrepreneurs to build "postproduction" facilities such as Hollywood's Post Group to service such television shows as *Star Trek: The Next Generation*. The Post Group also opened a branch at Disney-MGM to work on *Superboy*, and provide the digital effects and graphics, computer animation, and electronic editing services the series required.

"We'll apply whatever we learned from the films and combine it with what they can do at Post Group," Ilya Salkind explained in 1988. "And they can do unbelievable things. And what we're getting is very exciting."

Production of *Superboy* combined the best of traditional and new methodologies: 35mm filming and digital post. Manufacturers and developers of the early digital post systems used *Superboy* to test and refine their systems. Chief among these companies were Digital F/X for electronically painting out wires and compositing motion imagery, computer-based editing systems such as the CMX 9000 and the Ediflex, and the New England Digital Synclavier TS Direct-to-Disk audio-editing system.

After its debut in October 1988, *Superboy* quickly became the country's number-one first-run weekly syndicated television series, airing in 170 markets, representing 96 percent of the U.S.A. Distributed by Viacom Enterprises, *Superboy* was typically telecast during late afternoons and early evenings, providing advertisers with a means of reaching young-adult audiences, a valuable demographic amid proliferating cable channels, "superstations," direct-satellite services, and other new viewing options such as consumer VCR's, which had greatly diversified the television viewing landscape.

Superboy provided Disney-MGM with a high-profile weekly series to demonstrate what it and its in-house Post Group facility could achieve. From its second season onward, the series moved to nearby Universal Studios/Florida, which offered expanded space and greater postproduction capabilities at its onsite Century III Teleproductions facility. Retitled *The Adventures of Superboy* in its third season, with new producer Julia Pistor, the series continued to maintain a close working relationship with DC Comics, in New York. DC editors approved all scripts, several of which were penned by DC's own writers. The relationship was similar to the one that had existed more than 30 years earlier between DC Comics and its own Hollywood-based *Adventures of Superman* television production team.

Ironically, the very thing that made *The Adventures of Superboy* possible (the then-revolutionary—and relatively affordable—digital post and mastering solutions used to make the series), eventually turned into technical shortcomings for its future marketability. That's because television production and display technologies transitioned to digital high definition (HD) during the ensuing decade. Although photographed ("originated") on 35mm film, all of that footage was routinely scanned into standard definition (SD) video for editing and digital effects creation. Mastered in what soon became the obsolete SD D-2 videotape format, all *Superboy* episodes are now inferior to today's commonplace HD image quality. Broadcast-grade digital HD video capture and editing solutions did not become fully practical until circa 2000, narrowly missing Superboy by less than a decade.

Further hindering the show's modern-day visual appeal is the fact that its directors framed it in the traditional 4:3 aspect ratio (screen size) of broadcast television, as opposed to HDTV's widescreen 16:9. Whereas the 1950's *Adventures of Superman*—also shot in 4:3—could theoretically be transferred to HD because its finished episodes exist on 35mm film reels, finished *Adventures of Superboy* episodes were archived on obsolete D-2 videotape cassettes. The only way to visually "modernize" and "up-rez" *The Adventures of Superboy* would be to digitally scan the show's original 35mm camera negatives (if they still exist) to an HD image format and then re-create all digital effects in HD as well. "Fake" 16:9 widescreen could be achieved by cropping the top and bottom of the frame, but this is an undesirable compromise that loses a portion of valuable picture information and requires a slight increase in image size that can increase grain/picture noise and further soften the image. In any case, it would be cost-prohibitive in terms of time and labor.

The next television series to feature planet Krypton's Kal-el, *Lois & Clark: The New Adventures of Superman* (produced from 1993 to 1997), successfully anticipated the coming age of HDTV and made provisions for it. Produced by Warner Bros. in Hollywood, the series ignored *The Adventures of Superboy* continuity with a totally different approach that focused on the time-honored triangle of Lois, Clark, and Superman. I wrote a technical article on the making of this series in 1993 when I was the editor of *Videography* magazine. If the techo-speak thus far in this chapter hasn't caused you to bail, this article—reproduced here in its entirety—probably will. If not, you're a *very* dedicated Superman fan.

A Digital Job for Superman
"Look! Up in the sky! It's a bird, it's a plane, it's _____ !"

Is there *anyone* who can't fill-in that blank? Probably not. And therein lies the challenge of post and effects for *Lois & Clark: The New Adventures of Superman.*

As its title suggests, this new Warner Bros. Television/ABC series focuses on American pop culture's most famous love triangle. But although it's a "relationship" show, Superman's 55-year career in comic books, radio, serials, TV, Broadway, and movies has conditioned audiences to expect amazing visuals. To make sure nobody's disappointed, Warner Bros. turned to Santa Monica CA based Digital Magic, which not only produced effects far beyond those of mortal facilities, but also conformed the pilot episode in 4:3 and 16:9 D-1 video and output the effects to film for PAL release and theatrical exhibition overseas.

"Part of the challenge was the nature of the project," explains Elan Soltes, *Lois & Clark*'s Visual Effects Supervisor. "It's Superman, so people have a lot of expectations about what they want to see. And just as we were about to start the pilot the studio decided that everything needed to be done in 16:9. I sometimes feel I could travel the country just doing 16:9 workshops, because it can be hard for people to understand. But for us it made a lot of things possible and opened up film-output options."

Shot in 35mm at Warner Bros. by Roundelay Productions, *Lois & Clark*'s pilot episode included computer-generated imaging (CGI) by Vision Art and miniatures and special live-action elements filmed at Praxis/The Site. Digital Magic, which also does effects for *Deep Space Nine* and *Star Trek: The Next Generation*, among other shows, performed compositing and digital effects on the pilot and continues to work on the series, supplying all telecine, digital effects, and compositing.

"The show touches every service we have: telecine, Paintbox, editing, compositing, playback effects," explains Jeff Beaulieu, Executive Producer for Digital Magic Studios. "Everything had to be monitored in the 16:9 mode, so we started a vocabulary list for 16:9 that Warner Bros. would recognize. All of their producers and engineers got together to talk to our producers, engineers, and artists. Some of our staff have film backgrounds, so they understood that when operations got a phone call asking for a shot in 'squeeze mode' or 'unsqueezed mode' we all had to talk the same language. Since we're talking 16:9—not anamorphic— what the producers really meant was they wanted to see it in 1.33:1 [4:3]. We can't call it that, however, because we were running it through digital effects systems, so we had different specific names for things. The first week of dailies flew by without a hitch. Then we were doing the effects and there wasn't a problem whatsoever."

"Not only do they have an already cut D-1 16:9 copy of the pilot but they're also cutting negative," Beaulieu adds. "All our effects for *Lois & Clark* have to go back to film. Digital Magic's Vision Magic process, which includes its own proprietary software and Solitaire film recorders, can go to 2,000-line resolution film. It's been used for *Dracula*, *Cliffhanger*, and *The Sandlot*."

"We transferred the dailies 16:9 to D-1 [for the pilot] because Warner wants it done this way. The show was so effects-laden all the effects had to be monitored in 16:9. After we were done we ran it through an Abekas A57, which then provided the 1.33:1 aspect ratio for television release. The series will be done 16:9 too. We adjusted monitors in telecine to that mode, and we have 16:9 monitors in the bays."

"We made the color look very natural," explains Colorist Michael Mazur, who transfers original camera negative for the series. "We have a Rank Turbo II and Pogle color corrector with the Digital Color Processor, providing an all-digital path straight to D-1 for the pilot and Betacam SP for the episodes. We have a SteadiGate II, which I feel is quicker and more reliable than other mechanical or electronic pin-registration systems. Lynette Duensing does all effects transfers for shots that are going to be composited.

"It took some time to get used to seeing the images in 16:9 while transferring," Mazur says. "After everything was composited 16:9 it was then digitally copied for the air dub in 4:3."

"Essentially we did all shots twice," Soltes elaborates. "I don't necessarily mean shooting or compositing twice, but we made sure everything was put together in what we called a 30-frame version, or a frame-for-frame, video-for-film-output version. And then once the shots were completed we would stretch them out to a 24-frame version, or to a TV version. In other words adding a pulldown into the composited shots."

"We had all effects material [on the pilot] transferred at 30 frames per second rather than 24. It was transferred to D-1 with no pulldown; one frame of film equaled one frame of video. For roto sequences it means that there's 20 percent fewer frames to roto. Harry [the Quantel effects system] has a cine-expand feature so that when you output from it back to tape you can put a pulldown back into the shot.

"The same thing was done in the bay, where we worked with shots at 30 frames, or one frame of shot film to one frame of video. Then that stuff was essentially archived at 30 frames, and then also expanded out again through the Abekas A64 disk recorders, which are able to put in a digital pulldown.

"What it all means," Soltes adds, "is that when the show goes through our Vision Magic software for the Solitaire film recorder, a digital frame of composited information on video medium translates to a frame of film. There's no artifacts, no field motion, and it eliminates a lot of the problems of video being transferred to film."

The theatrical version of the *Lois & Clark* pilot, destined for exhibition in Europe and Asia, will continue the trend of movies that rely heavily on electronic imaging. Janet Muswell is one of several Visual Effects Compositors to work on the pilot (others are Pat Clancy and Scott Rader; Visual Effects Animators include Adam Howard, Steve Scott, and Simon Holden; Laurel Resnick is Visual Effects Artist). As Muswell explains, the project took advantage of the full Digital Magic arsenal.

"We used Sony's System G extensively," she says, "along with the Abekas A84 switcher and A57 effects system. System G is nice equipment to use in two dimensions, but you can also get some great effects with it that basically look like computer-generated 3-D, and for much less money and time. We did some shots on System G that everyone *thought* were computer-generated, but weren't."

"We did a globe where Superman flies to China to get take-away dinners," Muswell says, citing an example. "I was able to do a very quick, half-hour test with a flat version of the shot, showing all the motion, which the producers approved. We never had to go back; everyone saw it before we had it composited."

"I did the final by importing six [map] panels of the world into our Quantel Paintbox and cleaning them up. Then I stuck them together in System G, composited the background, and lined them up so the text and every layer was very clear. Harry was used to do a trail of Superman flying across the world."

Flying is, of course, what audiences think of first and foremost with Superman. To accomplish that feat, Actor Dean Cain was photographed in front of a green screen, footage of which was combined with aerial shots on the A84's digital chroma keyer. "They're pretty damned good," Muswell says of those keyers, and adds that it's often tricky to make this illusion believable.

"It's difficult sometimes to get the daytime aerial-type footage in the background to match with Superman. It has to be lit correctly; if it was a dull day when they shot the background, Superman has to be lit with dull lighting coming from the correct angle. Shots where he's very small can be difficult because when he goes between the scanlines you get aliasing. That's one of the reasons we used CGI in the pilot."

Vision Art's CGI work on *Lois & Clark* might be ironically described as invisible CGI. Audiences *expect* Superman to fly, but getting an actor in harness to soar out a window and disappear into a distant speck—all in one continuous shot—is physically impossible. Vision Art's solution was to morph the live-action Superman into an exact CGI duplicate. Whereas audiences have been thrilled by movies where people turn into liquid-metal robots or panthers, this morph is invisible, the effect potentially taken for granted as something natural to the character.

"A live-action-to-CGI morph is something the human eye could detect immediately if not done right," explains Josh Rose, Production Manager at Vision Art, in Santa Monica. "It's very complicated to disguise and basically has never been done for TV. Our animators joke that if they're doing their job right nobody knows they did anything."

Vision Art employed Silicon Graphics Inc. R4000 and R3000 Indigo workstations with software by Toronto-based Side Effects (Prisms for 3-D modeling and animation; Mojo for morphing) to morph Clark Kent as he flew out of an alley, and also to turn a live-action Superman into CGI as he soared out a window. The real secret of these transformations, Rose reveals, was a precise database of the actor's body.

"Cain was flown to Cyberware (Monterey CA), which did a 3-D scan of him to give us a base model to work with," Rose explains. "They sat him down and a laser went all the way around him. This data was then sent back with Cain and loaded into our system. The digitized body doesn't have any joints. It's just a foundation—arms, legs, chest, and head—to build on. We put it all together; joints had to be made so body parts could move. There was a pretty intensive amount of body development over six weeks. We made three of them: a Superman body, a Clark Kent suit coat body for the alley scene, and a trench coat body that didn't make it into the pilot.

"The morph occurs over 24 frames," Rose says of the actual effect, "because we produce everything at 24 frames and then a pulldown is added into it for video. In that 24 frames we had at least 12 keyframes; most morphs end up having only a few to make them work. Basically we had to have the extras because going from live action to CGI is not an easy task.

"We won an Emmy last year for creating Odo, a character in *Deep Space Nine*," Rose concludes. "I just hope we don't get ignored next year for *Lois & Clark* because you can't tell what we did!"

Assembly of the show's various elements begins with Digital Magic's transfer and shipment of all dailies to the Warner Bros. lot. There, Editors such as Ed Salier use a trio of Avid model 4000 Media Composers to offline the show for producer approval. "I haven't heard any complaints," says Associate Producer Tony Palermo concerning the use of digitized offline video on the Warner lot. "I was pretty impressed the first time I saw an Avid demo."

Audio post is handled on Warner's dubbing stages using the Digital F/X CyberFrame. "I love it," says Palermo of that particular digital audio workstation. "I think it's wonderful. I'm waiting for the day when we have the stages built so that we can actually plug those things in on the stage and make changes right there."

Audio for the show is recorded on Fostex PD-2 DAT machines by Sound Engineer Ken Fuller. "We use an analog Nagra for backup, but we're looking for that cleaner, digital sound," Palermo explains. "Ken is very meticulous and does an excellent job. I've actually had complaints that the dailies are *too* quiet and *lacked* noise."

"The Avids give an output of the audio, tracing the timecode back to the DAT. So therefore with the WaveFrame we can just put in the DATs and actually autoassemble the audio right there instead of having someone go in and hand-sync everything."

Upon producer approval, EDLs and 3/4-in. chase cassettes output by the Avids are sent back to Digital Magic for final Betacam SP-to-D-1 tape-to-tape transfer, color correction, and online assembly on a CMX Omni system.

"I'm really glad we rarely had to cut corners on this show," Soltes concludes. "The argument consistently was that 'people are going to have a lot of expectations about this, especially at 8 o'clock on a Sunday night.' But the most fun I had was looking at it when it was all done in its final composited version, with sweetened audio, on a 16:9 monitor. I realized then that we were looking at it like no one else in the country will see it for some time. Sixteen by nine has really changed my view of television. I want one. It was a lot of fun working in widescreen."

Smallville and Beyond

By 2001, when *Smallville* premiered on The WB Television Network, the integration of live-action 35mm cinematography, digital effects, and photorealistic computer animation had matured into a fine and seamless art. Anything a scriptwriter or director could imagine could pretty well be rendered onscreen—in HD—and at an affordable cost. With 217 hour-long (42-minute) episodes produced over the course of ten years, *Smallville* stands today as the longest-lived live-action Superman adaptation yet. The theatrical feature *Superman Returns* was produced and released during *Smallville*'s run, in 2006, marking the first time two different live-action versions of Superman appeared at the same time. *Superman Returns* made even more extensive use of photorealistic computer animation than ever before, with some flying shots of actor Brandon Routh actually created in a computer, as opposed to being captured by a camera. And the cameras that were used on this movie didn't even contain film, recording their imagery instead on HD videocassettes; these digital cinema camcorders were made by Sony and modified by Panavision.

Man of Steel followed seven years later, introducing actor Henry Cavill as Superman. Director Zack Snyder used 35mm film cameras but made extensive use of digital effects imaging and photorealistic computer animation. He also employed radical use of digital color-grading to imbue the film with a dark look that many fans found objectionable. Cavill's Superman uniform was a marked departure from previous Superman costumes, eliminating the traditional red trunks and prompting divisive opinions between older and younger Superman fans. Two sequels followed, in 2016 and 2017. The costume changes and dark tones were continued on the *Superman & Lois* television series, which debuted in 2021.

Also included in Superman's screen history are multiple animated television series produced since 1966 and more than a dozen direct-to-video animated features. All are worthy of study and—like their live-action counterparts—reflect advances in production technology that have improved the storytelling capabilities of each.

BRIAN MCKERNAN

Chapter Eight

Interview with Gerard Christopher

Superboy marked an historic return to live-action television for the Man of Steel when the show premiered October 3, 1988. It had been more than 30 years since the cameras rolled on "All That Glitters," the last episode of the *Adventures of Superman* and, like its historic predecessor, this new show was also a half-hour first-run syndicated action/adventure series featuring what was, at the time, state-of-the art special effects and a varied assortment of guest stars.

Totaling 104 episodes when production ended in late 1992, *Superboy* (retitled *The Adventures of Superboy* in its third and fourth seasons) was produced in Orlando, Florida, first at Disney/MGM Studios and then at Universal Studios/Florida. A co-production of Viacom and Alexander and Ilya Salkind (creators of the first three Christopher Reeve Superman movies and *Supergirl*), the show was well received among television critics and ranked among the top ten Nielson-rated new syndicated programs.

The show's first two seasons chronicled Superman's college years at Shuster University's Siegel College of Journalism (a nod to Superman's co-creators, Jerry Siegel and Joe Shuster). The equally fictitious Capitol City was the show's setting in its third and fourth seasons, in which Clark Kent and Lana Lang (Stacy Haiduk) completed their education with internships at the "Bureau for Extranormal Matters." These later episodes were executive produced by Julia Pistor for Lowry Productions.

Gerard Christopher, educated at New York's prestigious Julliard School and a veteran of many film and television roles, was selected for the coveted role of the young Superman after the departure of first-season lead John Haymes Newton. Over the course of Christopher's involvement with the series, he expanded his duties to become a producer and,

Credit: Patsy DiNome

Gerard Christopher let his brother Anthony try on a Superboy costume during a visit to Universal Studios/Florida.

on two occasions, scriptwriter. This interview is from 1994, and was originally done for Jim Nolt's *The Adventures Continue* fanzine, which was dedicated to *The Adventures of Superman* television series, hence the emphasis on that earlier series in this conversation.

McKernan: Was *The Adventures of Superman* on television in your home when you were growing up?

Christopher: I grew up with Superman and he's a real slice of American culture. When I was a child, George Reeves was the Superman I saw first. My upbringing was similar to that of most people; my mother told me I used to put a towel around my neck and jump off the roof of the garage in our back yard when I was a kid. When I got the role of Superboy I was pretty numbed by it. It's not like doing any other characters. Roles come and go, I worked on *Melrose Place* recently, but Superman is something that will always linger with me.

McKernan: Why?

Christopher: Because Superman is etched into television history. It's a real piece of American culture. It was a pretty awesome thing to do, to see the effect this character has on kids—on all people—all over the world. It was a little bit scary, but also a lot of fun. I got a lot of participation from fans who sent me the most unbelievable letters and were incredibly knowledgeable about the history of Superman. They told me some of the most obscure things that were just amazing. And it turned into a great experience for me, one that I couldn't have imagined when I started out. It was pretty daunting, just to fit in some way into the whole mold of what's been created in the Superman legend. It was amazing—a fantastic experience.

McKernan: I imagine that there were certain things that people expected to see—such as flying, which you did a lot of.

Christopher: And the reason I did was because of the fan mail. When I read letters the one thing people wanted to see—hands down—was flying. You could punch anything, break through walls, use X-ray vision, use heat vision—just as long as you show flying. Everyone loves it.

I looked to the best available examples of Superman in preparing for the role. I'd grown up with George Reeves' series, of course, and I looked at most of the other live-action versions: the Salkind movies, the serials with Kirk Alyn, and even the *Superboy* pilot done in 1961 with John Rockwell, who's actually a friend of mine. I never even knew he had been an actor until I got the *Superboy* series.

McKernan: Who particularly stands out among the other actors who have portrayed Superman?

Christopher: Like a lot of people, I have an emotional, sentimental attachment to what George Reeves did. He just seemed to do Superman the right way, the correct way, the way Superman is supposed to be done. I also have a lot of respect for the personality that Christopher Reeve brought to his Superman role. He's a big, tall, handsome guy and he gave the role a new twist and reawakened it. But in terms of sentimentality George Reeves is my favorite. I'd have to say I like them both.

McKernan: So seeing what others had done with your character was part of your research for the role?

Christopher: Yes, but there's something difficult about that, because you can't do what everyone else has done. You have to also make the role your own. That was a difficult thing to do because DC Comics had a very tight hold on us. There were many constraints as to what that character could and couldn't do. It was sometimes very difficult to have any kind of an ease about the character. But it was still a lot of fun. The word I get is that the cast of *Lois & Clark: The New Adventures of Superman* is having a bit more fun and is able to associate loosely on the set. They have more latitude because Warner Brothers, DC's parent, is overseeing things.

McKernan: Were you involved with the production of *Lois & Clark*?

Christopher: I actually read for the show. It was interesting. At first the casting director didn't like my interpretation. Then she asked me to change it. I did and she liked it. Then she brought me in to meet the producers. When I walked into the room, they had no advance knowledge that I had done *Superboy*.

Now, there are two ways to look at that: They're either going to love it because I had done the part before, or the opposite would be true—they'd hate it. I read for the producer and his reaction was, "Wow! You're great, it's wonderful, you're the perfect guy for this!" There was a room of six or eight people, it was kind of exciting. Then he grabbed my resume, looked at the work I'd done, flipped it over and said, "You've *done* this already!" He threw my resume down on the table and basically threw me out of the room. It was pretty funny.

You have to keep in mind the situation that the *Lois & Clark* people were in. It's similar to when a restaurant goes out of business and is taken over by new owners: The new management wants to change the decor, the menu, the colors, the fabrics on the chairs—everything. He could have looked at the new show as an easy transition for me—from Superboy to Superman. I'm older, I'm experienced, and I have a following. But he was making a big move, a big transition in how the character would be interpreted. He wanted to go a different way. People like to do things their own way and often times they cut ties with anything that came before for their own personal reasons. I'm not making any judgments; if that's what he wants to do it's his business.

McKernan: Are there any particular episodes of George Reeves' *Adventures of Superman* that stick in your mind?

Christopher: I like the ones that are mysterious. "Dagger Island," where he was on a deserted island. And "The Mysterious Cube," where he transmigrates through solid objects—I kind of regret that we didn't use that idea on *Superboy*.

I also like the pilot, "The Unknown People," with the Mole Men—it's just so weird. It also has Superman dealing with a worldwide issue, as opposed to just rescuing Lois when she's tied to some train tracks. It made me think, when I wrote episodes of *Superboy*, to created situations that put him in a world arena, not a local one. Here's a guy with all this power—what would he do *if...*?

McKernan: "Wish for Armageddon," one of the *Superboy* episodes you wrote, put him in that world arena, battling a force seeking global destruction. *Superboy* fills in the gaps of the Man of Steel's college years with a variety of stories that range from gritty crime tales to pure science fiction—similar to *Adventures of Superman* three decades earlier.

"Superboy...Lost" was clearly inspired by *Adventures of Superman*'s "Panic in the Sky," an episode recently remade again as a *Lois & Clark* installment ["All Shook Up"]. Superboy seemed to broaden in scope when you and producer Julia Pistor came on the scene.

Christopher: I owe my undying gratitude to Ilya Salkind for hiring and believing in me. Julia came in with fresh ideas and allowed me to make the changes I wanted to make. When she joined us we started getting some great episodes—we explored some interesting things and we had a lot of fun. Julia is a wonderful person and I can't say enough about her. She's very professional and she did what a producer has to do.

McKernan: The episode "Paranoia" was dark, yet funny, and guest starred Jack Larson and Noel Neill. It was very much an homage to *The Adventures of Superman*, with Larson saying "Jeepers!" at one point and making reference to having worked at a newspaper. What was it like to work with them?

Christopher: Right off the top, I have to say that Jack and Noel are a great pleasure to work with, it was really exciting. So many of the people on the *Superboy* crew grew up with *The Adventures of Superman* that it was very exciting for everybody. We were all in awe of them. Noel Neill is great. I felt that she was very appreciative to be there and that people wanted her. It was nice to work with her. She's a super lady. Jack Larson is a super guy, I can't say enough about him either. He's been personally helpful to me, career-wise, and he's an incredibly nice and generous person. He's got a great sense of humor. Jack kind of looks at the cockeyed side of life sometimes, and always has a laugh under his voice.

On the set, Jack was nice enough to say he thought our show was superior to his, which was sweet of him. He also said they never anticipated what a hit *The Adventures of Superman* would be back when he first got involved in it. He did it on a whim, never realizing that he'd get socked into it for seven years.

McKernan: Did Jack Larson and Noel Neill talk about George Reeves?

Christopher: They put the past in perspective in terms of their lives and careers. They just seemed to be having a lot of fun, which I was grateful for. That's part of the deal, having fun when we're working, and Jack added a lot to that.

I did talk to Jack about George Reeves. He recalled what a great guy George was. Very upbeat. Obviously, that's the word that's around about George to this very day—what an incredibly generous guy he was. George used to go around putting $100 bills in other actors' hands and telling them, "Now go make a million!"

McKernan: Aside from Jack Larson and Noel Neill, who were the most interesting guest stars you worked with on *Superboy*?

Christopher: The one that really stands out for me is Ron Ely ("The Road to Hell, Part 2"). In terms of an actor and a man, he is one of the most interesting, dynamic, intelligent, and personable individuals I've ever met. I was very impressed by him.

George Lazenby ("Abandon Earth," "Escape to Earth") was probably the person I had the most fun with. He's one of the most naturally funny and charming people you'll ever meet. He has amazing grace and charm.

McKernan: What did it feel like when *Superboy* ended its production run?

Christopher: It was sad. I hate to say it, but when you work that closely with people on the set it's like you're married to all 110 of them. There was a sense of completion because we knew and anticipated the end of the show's production schedule. We were able to kind of set ourselves up for the end psychologically, and do things that we wanted to do, which was fun. But it was sad. We were all ticking down the days. We worked almost one continuous year with very few breaks. People feel burned out when they're working twelve hours a day, and often longer. We'd get all stressed out, but I'd tell people, "We're all going to miss this, don't forget it." Sure enough, it's all people talk about now. You wouldn't know it, but the behind-the-scenes aspects of the show were really nice.

McKernan: In what way?

Christopher: The staff and the production value was nice, the quality of the treatment of actors and people—all of that was of very high quality. There are a lot of personal relationships that will go on. Professionally it was the most incredible experience for me to work with a lot of older, famous actors, some wonderful directors, and to learn a lot, get a directing contract, and to write and end up producing the show. I got the full boat on that show—I was lucky. It was tough to leave it.

McKernan: Any closing thoughts?

Christopher: Just that *The Adventures of Superman* and George Reeves both had a great effect on me, and on the work I did in *The Adventures of Superboy*. And that's important.

McKernan: I'd say that *Adventures of Superman* had a great effect on everyone born since 1951.

Christopher: Yes, George Reeves portrayed a major, honest hero. And when you think of what people are watching today! *The Adventures of Superman* was a big deal. Japanese Emperor Hirohito was a great fan of the show and used to send fan letters to George Reeves. It was done at a time in history when America was at a height. The show kind of fed all of that, there was so much going on. America was at the pinnacle of its strength in the world, those were interesting times.

There's honesty in George Reeves' Superman. And strength tempered with humility. It's fun.

Chapter Nine

Nick-at-Nite's Superman Night

The news was too good to be true. Nick-at-Nite, the Viacom cable network that programs for the "thirtysomething" generation with such classic television shows as *Get Smart*, *F-Troop*, and *Dragnet* was adding *The Adventures of Superman* to its lineup. Not only that, but they planned to kick off the series with a three-day marathon that would include mint-condition prints of the Technicolor Fleischer/Famous Studios Superman cartoons and episodes of the Columbia Pictures Kirk Alyn Superman movie serials. Best of all, however, was the news that on September 19, 1991, in celebration of adding the series to its schedule, Nick-at-Nite was going to present a theatrical screening of *Superman and the Mole Men*, the first in 40 years.

True, Warner Home Video had located the master positive of *Mole Men* in 1987 and released it that year on VHS for Superman's fiftieth birthday. But *this* screening would literally offer the "look and feel" of the film's original theatrical presentation. Wide World Cinemas, an upscale multiscreen Manhattan movie house, was selected as the site for the special evening. And special it was!

"Superman is something that appeals to all ages because everybody—no matter how old they are—grew up with him and knows who he is," explains Larry Jones, Publicity Director at the MTV Networks, which includes Nick-at-Nite. "We wanted to do something special to mark the addition of *Superman* to Nick's schedule, and this seemed like a good idea."

Number-one Superman collector Jim Hambrick was flown in from Southern California for the event to display part of his amazing wares, including an extremely rare George Reeves black & white costume, a Reeves color costume, the namesake prop of the episode "The Man in the Lead Mask" (1953), original rubber skull caps from *Superman and The Mole Men*, a one-and-only Reeves life mask (created for makeup needs), and many other one-of-a-kind items. Hambrick set up his collection in and around an unused ticket booth in the theater's extensive mezzanine. He even had original *Mole Men* posters, which fit perfectly in the glass display cases lining the hall outside the screening room. Danny Fuchs, renowned New York Superman collector, met Hambrick early in the day at the theater and together they set up the displays. At 5:30pm the doors opened for the invitation-only audience.

Although people stood three and four deep to marvel at Hambrick's collection, the star attractions of the evening were Phyllis Coates and Jack Larson, television's original Lois Lane and Jimmy Olsen. Together they posed for photographs with invited guests beside 3 ft. by 4 ft. blowups of their official television series portraits and Hambrick's life-size wax George Reeves Superman figure. As they have so many times before, but with no less the enthusiasm, Coates and Larson recalled for interviewers the great pleasure it was to have worked with Reeves, and the fine individual that he was. They spoke of the sense of fulfillment they feel today for having been involved in this phenomenally successful series, which, with *I Love Lucy* and *The Honeymooners*, constitutes the longest success stories in television history.

As show time approached, the mezzanine and theater lobby filled to capacity. Upon entering, guests were greeted at a table where green "Krypton Cocktails" were served. Table decorations of crystal-like green Plexiglas were clearly inspired by production designer John Barry's work on the Christopher Reeve Superman movies. Further down the mezzanine, across from Hambrick's display, and toward the two screening rooms that would be showing *Mole Men* was a table of hors d'oeuvres that included a large rendering of the Superman "S" symbol done in red, yellow, and black ravioli. Nick-at-Nite/Viacom executives

Author Brian McKernan plays Clark Kent with *Adventures of Superman* actors Jack Larson (Jimmy Olsen) and Phyllis Coates (Lois Lane of the series' first 26 episodes).

and employees mingled with advertisers, media representatives, and DC Comics staffers. DC folk included VP Paul Levitz, Superman artist/ writer John Byrne, and noted retirees such as editor Julius Schwartz and artist Murphy Anderson.

Pop music played over the house PA system, featuring such recordings as The Kinks' "(Wish I Could Fly) Like Superman" and REM's "Superman" song. Weaving their way amid the crowd as ushers were three tuxedoed "Mole Men," professional actor/models hired for the occasion who also happen to be little people. Like Billy Curtis, Jack Banbury, Jerry Marvin, and Tony Baris from the 1951 movie, these "Mole Men" were the true supermen that made the event "work." For over an hour (while wearing bald rubber skull caps and monster glove-hands) they ad-libbed pantomimes with the guests, posed for photos, and generally lent just the right "quirkiness" to the occasion to get everyone in the mood for a film that was out of the ordinary. Nodding to a 1950s movie-publicity technique, the Nick-at-Nite folks also had a "nurse" on hand with a stethoscope in case someone was "overcome with fright," as the character Pop Shannon (veteran actor J. Farrell MacDonald) was in the film after first sighting the weird subterranean creatures.

The curtain went up at 7pm sharp, and after a raffle for Nick-at-Nite Superman plates and a showing of an episode of the then-new Nick series *Rugrats*, *Superman and the Mole Men* began. A cautionary tale of small-town intolerance, *Mole Men* is a timeless tale of fear and moral cowardice versus courage and understanding. Some of the dialogue, written in a more innocent age, provoked unintended laughs, but the film's message of tolerance hit home in a city recently shocked by the stabbing death of an innocent young rabbinical student by an angry mob bent on revenge.

It's important to note that before *The Adventures of Superman* ever appeared on television it was also a long-running radio program. Racial and ethnic tolerance was a frequent theme of the radio scripts (see Chapter Four), and producer Robert Maxwell, who oversaw the show's transition from radio to television, clearly drew upon this essential aspect of "Truth, Justice, and the American Way" as the theme for *Mole Men*. Maxwell, under the pseudonym Richard Fielding, co-wrote the screenplay for the film (with DC Comics' then-editorial director Whitney Ellsworth), which would serve as the pilot for the television series (and later be included as its only two-part episode, renamed "The Unknown People"). Maxwell also co-produced (with Bernard Luber) *The Adventures of Superman*'s first season, sharing the "Fielding" name with Ellsworth on three episodes.

On the occasion of the film's 1987 video release, *Village Voice* critic Richard Goldstein commented that watching *Superman and the Mole Men* "is like opening a time capsule from 1951—the air inside may be musty, but it's cleaner than anything we've been breathing lately." He praised what he called a "dark, nasty thriller."

"One result of Maxwell's toughness is that the movie holds up," Goldstein writes. "It's genuinely sinister, most notably in the vicious, bigoted attitudes of the townspeople, from working-class yobbos right up to the head of the local hospital." And he concludes that it's "a fascinating bit of history, screencraft, and pop culture, from an era of movies and kids' programming that most of us don't know or remember."

If anyone in the *Mole Men* audience had forgotten or didn't know about the film before it started, that wasn't the case when the lights went back up. As the audience filed out of the screening room they were handed commemorative sweatshirts (bearing a pictogram that reads "I saw *Superman and the Mole Men* on Nick-at-Nite"), and a good feeling pervaded that a lost classic had been restored. People filed out, taking last looks at Hambrick's collection as he and Fuchs began to pack it up for the journey back to California (it's now on permanent display at The Super Museum, in Metropolis, Illinois).

The following morning Coates and Larson appeared on *Live With Regis And Kathy Lee*, showing a clip from the series and reiterating the satisfaction they felt at having been a part of it. Thanks to Nick-at-Nite, an entire generation has discovered (or rediscovered) the work of Reeves, Maxwell, Luber, and Ellsworth. Prints are beautiful, and although the episodes are edited, all cuts are logical ones and the show isn't interrupted by extra commercials.

On Nick-at-Nite you can follow the evolution of the *Adventures of Superman*'s 104 episodes from stark and striking film noir of the 1951-3 episodes to the colorful "science-fictiony" episodes of 1954-7. *The Adventures of Superman* was the first TV show with special effects optically printed in motion-picture style; when viewed against *I Love Lucy* or *The Honeymooners*, it becomes immediately apparent that the show's budget was downright lavish for 1950s TV, and far ahead of its time. Nick-at-Nite and its parent company, Viacom, are to be congratulated for putting *The Adventures of Superman* back on television. They're supporting the show with an innovative batch of promos, including the whimsical "Jimmy Olsen 30-Minute Workout," a 30-second compilation of shots of Jack Larson being punched by villains in various episodes:

"Criminals of Metropolis: Nick-at-Nite knows that fighting Superman means staying in shape. But often you just don't have the time. That's why there's the 'Jimmy Olsen 30-Minute Workout.' No matter what shape you're in you can always get in a brisk upper-body workout by beating Jimmy up every night of the week. Only a special guy would take it on the chin for you. But that's just how much Jimmy cares. The Jimmy Olsen 30-Minute Workout; one more reason Metropolis thugs watch The Adventures of Superman, *weeknights at 8:30, 7:30 Central, on Nick-at-Nite!"*

Today, as a new Superman feature film is reportedly in preparation and Lorimar television announces a new live-action Superman TV series [*Lois & Clark*], producers of superhero cinema need only look toward *Superman and the Mole Men* for an example of how to do it right. The evening of September 19, 1991 was the beginning of a Superman renaissance.

Chapter Ten

Superman's Super DVD

There have been many DVD editions of Superman: The Movie *(and the other three Christopher Reeve Superman films) since its first release in that format in 2001. This article originally appeared in* DVDWorks *magazine in April 2001, and details the extraordinary measures taken to prepare a super DVD debut for* Superman: The Movie. *Since then, new footage has been discovered on all of these films, and even more definitive versions of* Superman: The Movie *(and its sequels) have been released on DVD (and Blu-ray Disc) editions. This article, however, presents an account of how the first big-budget Superman movie was mastered for DVD when the format was still in its "early days."*

One of the most popular and profitable films of all time, *Superman* won a special Oscar for visual effects, inspired several film sequels, and has been a TV syndication and VHS favorite for years. Now, however, the Man of Steel is getting DVD treatment, and Warner Home Video is planning a disc fit for a superhero.

The *Superman* DVD, slated for release later this year, will be a two-sided DVD-18 disc with a definitive director's cut, a brand-new digitally remixed 5.1 Surround soundtrack, three new documentaries, original trailers, screen tests, a commentary by director Richard Donner and screenwriter Tom Mankiewicz, special ROM content, and updatable web-enabled features. All told, the disc will contain nearly two hours of new visual material; its flip side features a remastered version of composer John Williams' original score, one of the first to be recorded in Dolby stereo.

"This DVD is a definitive director's cut that's really interesting because I've put material back that I never thought I would have the opportunity to," says Donner, also the director of the *Lethal Weapon* series, *The Omen*, and *Conspiracy Theory*. "It's very exciting. There's an additional scene of Marlon Brando no one's ever seen."

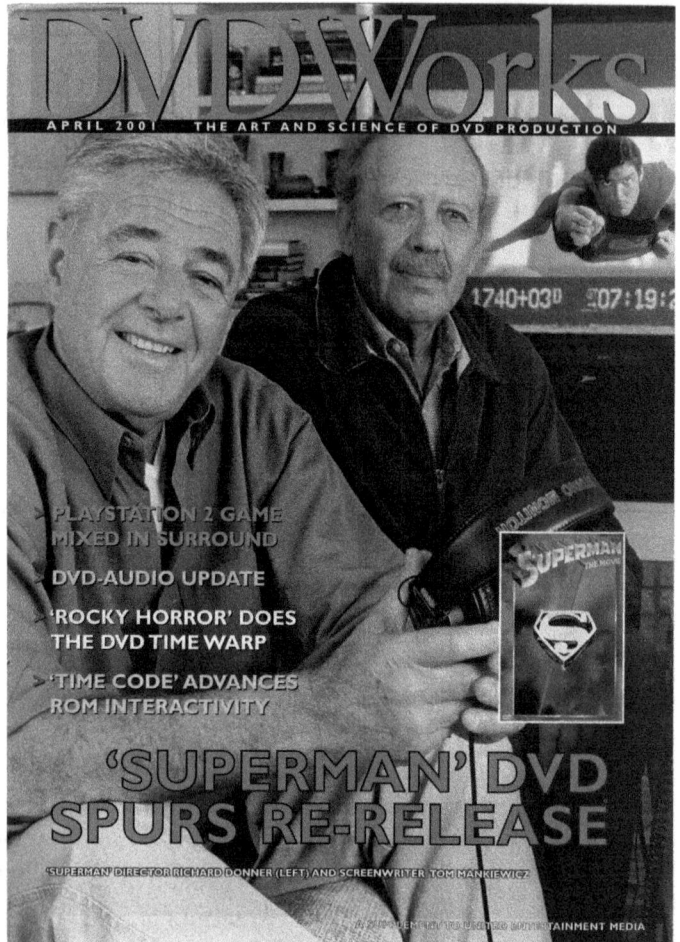

"Also, I wanted to get the DVD out there to help with publicity for Chris Reeve," Donner adds. "Not only are we bringing *Superman* into another generation, obviously, but there's an opportunity to get people to be more aware of Chris and his plight, and it's already starting to happen. I've gotten a lot of calls about it."

Finding the original sound and picture elements for the DVD version of *Superman* was the job of producer/editor Michael Thau, who searched

BRIAN MCKERNAN

the vaults of London's Pinewood Studios, where the film was shot and edited.

"When Michael Thau came to me with the ideal to do this DVD I said it'll be phenomenal, but I'll only do it if he'll be the one who makes it happen," Donner continues. "Michael is a very dedicated filmmaker, and he was quite magical in helping me do this."

Under Donner's supervision, Thau re-cut the film, every frame of which was cleaned by hand. He also re-mixed the soundtrack and oversaw the digital restoration of several shots. Creating this definitive cut, Donner explains, even prompted Warner Bros. to plan a special "preview weekend" in San Antonio TX on March 24. If successful, the studio will re-release *Superman* to movie theaters nationally in similar fashion to its wide re-release of *The Exorcist* (1974) last year.

"Warner got such a reaction on their website to the fact that the *Superman* DVD is coming that it provoked them into releasing it theatrically as well," Donner states. "They'll probably hold the release of the DVD until shortly after the release of the film so it will generate a lot of publicity for both."

Detective Work
One of the challenges of creating a DVD for a movie produced decades ago is the fact that the passage of time and re-edits for television versions can make locating the original footage difficult—or even impossible.

"You'll see my definitive cut, barring the fact that a lot of outtakes, negatives, printed lifts, and things like that never made it into the can in Los Angeles," Donner says. "There's been quite a lot of disappearances."

"There are two other cuts that existed," Thau elaborates, in addition to the theatrical cut. One was for an ABC telecast and the other was for TV syndication. "We sat down and looked at all the extra footage and [eventually] got down to a cut that's about ten minutes longer."

"All those extra scenes come from the ABC version, although [the DVD is] not the entire ABC version. There was good cut negative on those extra scenes. The audio for the ABC version was mono, though, so I had to find sound elements."

Although Warner Bros. had already shipped six tons of negatives, prints, and sound for *Superman* from England to Los Angeles, Thau found he had to go to London to seek out additional elements. The original theatrical negative, meanwhile, had been located and shipped to Warner Bros. from DeLuxe's Paris laboratory.

"When I was over in England I went to the vaults where they stored all the *Superman* stuff, and I tripped over lots of sound elements, and—here's the greatest thing—all the negative of the original documentary shoot," Thau recalls. "There was so much that was unused, because back in 1978 the producers and Warner Bros. didn't want to show people how they made a man fly. They thought it would be a good marketing ploy not to reveal those techniques. But they shot all that stuff anyway. Now it's newly uncovered and this DVD will be the first time it's seen."

"I co-produced three documentaries for this project with Jonathan Gaines, a DVD producer from a company called Acoustic Visions," Thau continues. "Two cover the making of the film, which are very heartfelt and include interviews with Chris Reeve. We got new interviews with everyone except for Brando. And then we also built a documentary around just the visual effects and amazing early effects test footage that they did in preproduction on the film. They didn't use video cameras back then, so everything was shot on film, and I have pretty good prints on a lot of that stuff."

Thau shot an interview with Roy Field, optical supervisor on *Superman* and one of the film's few surviving effects artists. Field acts as host of that documentary, and shows such never-before-seen footage as a test of a miniature remote-controlled flying Superman.

Transfer and Repair

Ancillary content aside, the most important consideration in mastering Donner's definitive *Superman* was preparing that original negative of the movie. The first step in this process entailed cleaning every frame by hand before transfer on a Philips Spirit DataCine and color-correction on a da Vinci 2K system.

"A guy wearing magnifying glasses sat with the negative, and picked hairs and dirt off it," Thau explains. "There were tears, scratches, and a lot of fading on CRI opticals, which I re-made."

Pacific Title digitally fixed a handful of flying shots, which were never quite right in the original film, made in the pre-digital age. For example, Superman's famous blue costume turned green in certain shots because its color was very similar to the blue-screen backing traditionally used in (analog film) motion-picture "traveling matte" effects.

"We couldn't compensate [color] in those days," Donner recalls. "Pac Title scanned-in the negative, digitally changed the green [costume] to blue, and then scanned it back out to negative," Thau says. "The DVD version looks twice as good as a film print, which is not to say that the film print isn't pretty impressive as well."

"Dave Ludwig, of Warner Bros. Video Operations, did all the work on the video transfer and color correction, which I supervised. He used every trick in the book to make it look spectacular. Warner Bros. Video Operations is at the cutting edge of technology because of the leadership of Ned Price [vice president of technical mastering operations]. He's the reason why Warner Bros. DVD products look so great."

A Composer's Foresight

The sound elements Thau stumbled over at Pinewood proved to be equally invaluable in creating the *Superman* DVD, as they enabled Warner Bros. principal mixer Steve Pederson to remix the film in 5.1 Surround Sound.

"I noticed there was a box from the vault labeled ONE-INCH MISCELLANEOUS MASTERS," Thau explains. "And when we opened it up we had no idea of what it was going to be. It said ANVIL STUDIOS on it, which is where composer John Williams recorded his original score. It said '1M3,' '6M2,' '4M5,' and I thought, *Wait a second; those are music-cue numbers. Could this really be...?*"

"I then realized that I was looking at hours and hours of Williams' original mix. And these weren't just his recordings—the 24-tracks, which we found later in England. These were the *mix-downs*. This was pristine music. Williams had mixed most cues down into two sets of left/center/rights. So I had six discrete music tracks to work with for every cue in the film. And that allowed us to make an honest-to-God 5.1 spread with the music for the DVD release—not a synthesized spread. Williams had actually mixed his music down to six tracks. When you watch the film it's all around you; there's different instrumentation coming from the back left, from the back right, from the center, and so on. We took the kind of care and time that you would with any brand-new feature film."

"You'll also be able to flip the DVD and listen to just the 5.1 music alone, without any volume moves—just the cues as they were recorded," Thau continues. "And we found some other cues that were in much longer versions; cues that have never been heard before. We included those as supplemental material at the end of the DVD in 5.1 as well."

Thau adds that these original mix-downs were recorded on one-inch analog tape in England. "Tape that old can go bad real quick," he says, "so as we played it back we immediately captured it in ProTools. We did these transfers at the big music-scoring stage at Warner Bros. Dan Leahy was the sound-effects mixer; he had the most work because we had to rebuild all the effects from scratch."

"I also found the original production sound from the dailies," Thau adds. "Unfortunately it would have been impossible to re-create all of the dialog because we didn't find all that looping, and there was a lot of it in that film. So there's certain scenes where we just take the original mono dialog stem and do the best we could with livening it up."

Up, Up, and Away

Upon completion of the *Superman* DVD's audio and video components, the next stop was the California Video Center, Warner's DVD authoring facility. There, digital compression, menuing, and QC will ensure the optimal viewing experience Donner and Thau intended.

With a new Superman feature film currently in preproduction and *Smallville*, a WB TV pilot based on Clark Kent's teenage years, shooting this month, Superman continues to be among the world's most enduring fictional characters. Given the care with which Donner, Thau, and their Warner Bros. colleagues have taken to exploit the excellent picture quality and increased storage capacity of DVD, the *Superman* disc seems certain to set a new standard of excellence in movie releases.

"Of all the popular films I've done—*The Omen*, the *Lethal Weapon* films, *Maverick*—nothing has prompted people to comment so much years later as *Superman* has," Donner reflects. "It's amazing, I never realized what I was getting myself into."

Chapter Eleven

Superman Bob Holiday

Question: Which actor holds the record for the most live-action performances as Superman? (I specify "live action" because radio actor Bud Collyer portrayed Superman more than 2,000 times on the airwaves from 1940 to 1950.)

Is the live-action Superman record-holder George Reeves, Dean Cain, Tom Welling, or Tyler Hoechlin on television? Is it Kirk Alyn, Christopher Reeve, Brandon Routh, or Henry Cavill in the movies? The answer is none of the above.

It's Bob Holiday, who portrayed Superman (and Clark Kent) live on stage and *flying* an estimated 200 times in the 1966 musical *"It's a Bird...It's a Plane...It's Superman."* The show premiered on Broadway at The Alvin (now Neil Simon) Theatre on March 29, 1966 after three months of Philadelphia and New York previews. The show closed on July 17, 1966 after 129 Broadway performances but was revived the following summer as nighttime open-air presentations drawing huge audiences at the St. Louis Municipal Opera and the Kansas City Starlight Theatre, again with Bob Holiday in the title role. Holiday also appeared on film as Superman in *The Story of Superman* (a mock newsreel shown during the play), in a color Aqua Velva aftershave commercial, and in an episode of the *I've Got a Secret* television game show.

Unfortunately, because no complete performance of the original 1966 Broadway production of *"It's a Bird...It's a Plane...It's Superman"* is known to have been captured on film or video, many of today's

BOB HOLIDAY

AS HE APPEARED
IN THE BROADWAY MUSICAL
"IT'S A BIRD . . . IT'S A PLANE . . .
IT'S SUPERMAN!"

Bob Holiday in costume in *"It's a Bird...It's a Plane...It's Superman"* (1966).

Superman fans are unfamiliar with Bob Holiday's place in Superman history. If they do know about the show it's most likely from seeing the YouTube post of a very disappointing video version that was produced by ABC-TV in 1975 with a totally different cast.

Nevertheless, record-holder Bob Holiday is the "missing link" between 1950's television Superman George Reeves and 1978-87 movie Superman Christopher Reeve. I had the good fortune to know Bob Holiday, and to have accompanied him to the 2003 Superman Celebration in Metropolis, Illinois. There, with producer Chuck Harter and director Steve McCracken, we filmed his visit as a guest celebrity for the documentary *Holiday in Metropolis*. Bob had retired from acting in 1978 to become a builder of resort homes in the Pocono Mountains region of Pennsylvania, but he was still a Superman at heart, a fan of the character since childhood. He also considered the other Superman actors as his "brothers," as he told audiences during his 2003 Metropolis stage performance.

"I grew up with Superman and the thrill of actually playing the part on Broadway was one of the most wonderful, greatest feelings I ever had in my life," Holiday told the audience. "I understand Superman very well. I understand the other men that played him very well. You can't know… what is in my head or what is in their heads unless you are the chosen one to play that part. I loved my role."

Although a DVD of the 1966 production of *"It's a Bird…It's a Plane… It's Superman"* can't be found at your local Walmart alongside Superman's movies and television series, the show's original cast album (in which Holiday sings three songs) has never been out of print, and has been released over the years as an LP record, an audiocassette, a CD, and on multiple streaming services. It's a show that is frequently revived by theatre companies large and small all over the world, with recent productions in New York, London, Los Angeles, Dallas, Australia, and Germany. The show is also enjoying increasing appreciation from a new generation of fans eager to learn about earlier Superman incarnations and the actor who originally played him on Broadway.

By the way, for legal reasons that nobody seems to understand, DC Comics stipulated back in 1966 that the word *Superman* should be at the end of the title, and that the entire title should be inside quotation marks. Luckily for DC Comics, they already had a well-known, ready-to-use title fitting these requirements that had long been part of the character's radio and television history, the phrase: *"It's a Bird…It's a Plane…It's Superman."* The use of this title somehow protects the name *Superman* from eventually going into the public domain. So even if the name of the show is set in *italic* type—the editorial style used by many magazines and books (including this one)—the quotation marks are still required. The title is presumably what Metropolis citizens exclaim when they see the Man of Steel flying above them. As for the ellipses (periods) used in the title, they appeared on the cover of the show's original Philadelphia *Playbill*, so we're using them here too.

Super Genesis
Turning Superman into a Broadway musical began in 1964 when composer Charles Strouse and lyricist Lee Adams (winners of a Tony Award three years earlier for *Bye Bye Birdie*) approached two young

Esquire magazine writers—David Newman and Robert Benton—about working together. Strouse and Adams were fans of the duo's annual Dubious Achievement Awards in *Esquire* and sought to tap their wit and creativity. The writers were stumped for ideas until Newman's wife Leslie spied a *Superman* comic book on the floor of their son Nathan's bedroom. Strouse and Adams loved the idea of a Superman musical, as did producer Hal Prince, who also agreed to direct it.

It wouldn't be Benton and the Newmans' last association with the Man of Steel; the trio later rewrote Mario Puzo's screenplay for *Superman: The Movie* (1978), and the Newmans went on to write two of that film's sequels. Newman and Benton also received an Oscar for their 1967 screenplay for the movie *Bonnie and Clyde*. Benton received a second Oscar 12 years later for directing and adapting the screenplay for *Kramer Vs. Kramer*.

Superman on Broadway seemed like a good bet in the mid-1960s. Comic-strip characters had provided inspiration for stage successes since *Bringing Up Father*'s Maggie and Jiggs in 1914, *The Yellow Kid* in 1920's vaudeville, and Broadway's *Li'l Abner* in 1956. By the mid-1960s the Pop Art craze was in full swing, with Andy Warhol appropriating ten-cent comic book drawings of Superman and turning them into highly valued artworks. The Man of Steel appeared in magazine ads for Continental Insurance in 1964 and would soon shill for *Newsweek* as well. Kids had long made his comic book titles bestsellers and adults no doubt noticed (and perhaps read) his syndicated daily newspaper strip, which began in 1939.

Satirist Jules Feiffer's landmark history *The Great Comic Book Heroes* rolled off the press in January 1965, sporting a big, bold Superman drawing on the cover. *The New York Sunday News Coloroto* magazine reported on June 6, 1966 that *The Adventures of Superman* television series (produced a decade earlier) was at the peak of its popularity even though its star George Reeves had died six years earlier. High ratings for this syndicated series prompted the American Broadcasting Company and 20th Century Fox to approach DC Comics about making an all-new live-action Superman for prime time. When they learned that Hal Prince had the rights, they opted to produce *Batman* instead for a January 1966 debut.

Macy's and Goodyear, meanwhile, were preparing a brand-new Superman helium balloon for the 1966 Thanksgiving Day parade. The first-ever paperback compendium of Superman comic-book stories debuted in 1966 from Signet Press. And out in Hollywood, Filmation Studios were producing Superman's first-ever made-for-television Saturday-morning animated cartoons, due to air on CBS that Fall. A pop-culture hero since his 1938 debut, Superman was soaring to even greater heights of popularity as 1966 dawned, and Broadway seemed his next likely conquest.

Possibilities

Newman and Benton's basic plot for *"It's a Bird...It's a Plane...It's Superman"* had mad scientist Dr. Abner Sedgwick secretly vowing to destroy "the world's symbol of goodness" (Superman) as revenge for being a "ten-time Nobel Prize-loser." Assisting Sedgwick is evil *Daily Planet* gossip columnist Max Mencken, who is jealous of Metropolis' love for Superman. Lois Lane, meanwhile, has all but given up hope that Superman will ever show a romantic interest in her, and is being courted by Sedgwick's handsome young assistant, Jim Morgan. Frustrated at being stood-up by Mencken one too many times, his "Girl Friday" Sydney targets Clark Kent as a romantic conquest, singing the show-stopping Strouse/Adams song "You've Got Possibilities" as she attempts to seduce him after-hours in the *Daily Planet* office. (The tune became a cabaret standard, later recorded by Peggy Lee and Joanie Sommers and also used in a 2005 Pillsbury Doughboy commercial.)

Casting *"It's a Bird...It's a Plane...It's Superman"* netted top talent, including veteran song-and-dance man Jack Cassidy as Max Mencken (a thinly disguised parody of notorious newspaper columnist Walter Winchell), gorgeous soprano Patricia Marand as Lois Lane, future *Alice* television star Linda Lavin as Mencken's neglected assistant Sydney, madcap Michael O'Sullivan as Dr. Abner Sedgwick, and Don Chastain as Jim Morgan.

Bob Holiday won the dual role of Superman and Clark Kent after he "survived rigorous physical tests that eliminated 51 competitors," according to *The New York Times* on November 17, 1965. The article added that the producer's specifications called for someone who stood 6 feet 4 inches, weighed 190 pounds, and had measurements of neck 17, chest 50, waist 32, hips 37 ½, biceps 18 ½, thigh 26 ½, and calf 17. "Mr. Prince conceded that the calf business was a joke," the *Times* added.

A Job For Superman

Thirty-three years old when he auditioned, Holiday's 6 foot, 4 inch, 190-pound frame, square-jawed good looks, and acting and singing abilities made him the perfect candidate to portray Broadway's Man of Steel. Born in Brooklyn in 1932, Holiday's introduction to show biz came when he was seven years old and visiting a Catskills resort with his mother. "There was an amateur contest, which I entered," he recalled. "I sang 'My Bonnie Lies Over the Ocean,' and I won. The prize was a lollipop. That was neat, and I wanted more lollipops, so I was bitten by the performing bug."

"When I was young, I loved comic books," Holiday noted in *Superman on Broadway*, his 2003 biography written with Chuck Harter. "I was a big Superman fan when I was a kid, and I remember the comic books very well. They were very real to me. As an only child, and a bit of a loner, Superman was a hero to me. Superman was a person who fought off evil, but was kind. He was tough, but he was gentle. When I say he was tough, he got you if you were the bad guy. He got you in a way that didn't destroy you, unless you had to be destroyed. He was a very lovable tough-guy. I did listen to the Superman radio show, and was mesmerized by the voice of Bud Collyer. It was great when Clark Kent would lower his voice and exclaim, '*This* is a job for Superman!'"

The future Superman went on to perform as a soloist in the George Washington High School glee club and appear on *The Ted Mack Amateur Hour* after graduation. Inspired by his heroes Dean Martin and Jerry Lewis, Holiday worked as a singer and comedian in Manhattan restaurants, joining the Army in 1953, where he polished his craft at NCO clubs and as a DJ on Armed Forces Radio in Germany. Holiday resumed his nightclub career after military service, performing in a variety of cities. In 1956 he worked as an MC at the Carousel Club, in Dallas, which was owned by Jack Ruby, later to become infamous as the killer of Lee Harvey Oswald, John F. Kennedy's assassin. Tall and handsome, Holiday found himself acting opposite such stars as Jayne Mansfield in 1963 at the Casino Royale in Washington DC. Later that year he enjoyed a two-minute kissing scene with Mamie Van Doren in a Westchester Dinner Theatre production of *Wildcat*. After being told to reduce the smooch to 30 seconds Holiday responded, "I'd rather take a pay cut."

Holiday's first major Broadway role was in *Fiorello!*, the Tony and Pulitzer Prize-winning 1959 musical by Jerry Bock and Sheldon Harnick directed by George Abbott (book by Abbott and Jerome Weidman). Playing the part of Neil, young law clerk opposite actor Tom Bosley as firebrand New York City mayor Fiorello LaGuardia, the show ran for 795 performances and provided Holiday with his introduction to producer Harold Prince. Road shows of *Camelot* and *Lady in the Dark* followed. Then came the Superman audition.

"I had a gut feeling I'd get the part, because I was a genuine Superman fan," Holiday recalled in *Superman on Broadway*. "At the end of the audition they dismissed another guy and told me I had the part. Hal Prince said he was very happy for me, and that this show was going to be a big hit. A chill went through me. I said, 'Thank you. Thank you.'"

"I relished that role," Holiday said years later, explaining that he felt a responsibility to uphold Superman's reputation, making time to meet with young autograph-seekers backstage after every performance. "I sign a big red S, tell them to drink their milk, and be good," he stated. "I got a big kick out of it."

Capelash

After months of rehearsals and previews in Philadelphia and New York, *"It's a Bird...It's a Plane...It's Superman"* opened to rave reviews. Stanley Kauffmann of *The New York Times* wrote, "It is easily the best musical so far this season...it would be enjoyable in any season." WABC-TV reviewer Alan Jefferys called it, "The fun musical of the year." Over at *The New York Post*, Richard Watts, Jr. wrote, "The production is ingenious and it seems undoubtedly headed for box-office acclaim." "It's so damned good," agreed George Oppenheimer at *Newsday*. "*Superman* is a hit and how," added Stuart Klein at WNEW. Whitney Bolton of *The New York Morning Telegram* wrote of Holiday's performance, "the embodiment of Superman makes the show come alive and sparkle. His portrait of a ponderous human miracle, in love with good deeds and unabashed virtue, is delightful."

Featuring innovative staging (including performers singing inside of multi-level open-front "cubes" simulating the look of comic-book cartoon panels), the show featured Holiday flying on wires into and out of various scenes. Flying By Foy, the world's leading theatrical flying experts, built the system that was used. "The flying harness was made of light leather," Holiday explained in *Superman on Broadway*. "It was attached around the chest, the upper arms, and down the back. I don't ever remember being afraid of flying on the wire. During performances I would back up slightly on stage, and an extra would unclip the wire. There were lots of hours of practice and those workouts at the gym really paid off. The only difficult part about the flying was keeping my legs extended on take off. I did it, but it was rough."

Holiday's biography also recalled the one performance when the wires broke: "I was flying in on an entrance, about six feet off the stage, when I felt this *crack* behind me. Thank God I had been working out, because I hit the stage and sprang back up again. I put my hands on my hips, looked straight at the audience, and said, *'That would hurt any mortal man!'* The audience screamed, cheered, and gave me a standing ovation."

Everybody loved Bob Holiday's Broadway flights, but *"It's a Bird...It's a Plane...It's Superman"* closed on July 17, 1966 after 129 performances. Co-writer Robert Benton attributed it to "capelash," noting that fellow DC Comics superhero *Batman* had debuted on ABC-TV just a few weeks before Superman arrived at The Alvin. Adult theatre audiences assumed the musical was just another campy *Batman* affair. *Why should I pay 12 bucks for a ticket to see Superman when I can watch* Batman *on television for free?* they reasoned. Adults also assumed it was strictly for kids, which it wasn't. The show had expanded to four sold-out matinees per week on June 29, 1966 to accommodate young audiences, but evening performances were plagued by empty seats. Also, the competition on Broadway was fierce that year, and it included original productions of some of the greatest hits in the history of the American musical theatre, including: *Sweet Charity, Mame, Cactus Flower, The Odd Couple, Man of La Mancha,* and *Fiddler on the Roof.*

A Fresh Start
Bob Holiday reprised his Superman role the following summer for limited engagements at the open-air St. Louis Municipal Opera and the Kansas City Starlight Theatre. He was the only original cast member, sharing the stage this time with such talents as Charles Nelson Reilly as the madcap Dr. Sedgwick. Before nighttime audiences estimated at 10,000, Holiday "flew," suspended 100 feet above the stage from a construction crane. "Looking back, I was taking quite a chance," Holiday recalled years later. "But when you're young you never think of those things."

He then headed for Hollywood, appearing in commercials, pilots, and auditioning for a planned television series called *The Brady Bunch.* "Sherwood Schwartz, the show's producer, told me that I had the lead role as the father," Holiday recalled in his biography. "I was ecstatic! Sherwood told me that he was convinced that this show was going to be a big hit. There were plans for the whole family at live musical gigs. I figured that this would open up Vegas for me."

"At the eleventh hour, Sherwood called me, practically in tears," Holiday continued. "He said the executives at ABC had overridden his decision to cast me. They had chosen Robert Reed for the part. He had been on a show called *The Defenders*, and was a known TV actor. I was devastated. Extremely disappointed. My big break had been yanked out from under me. I had to leave Hollywood, and in the very early 1970s I was back on the road in musical theatre."

Productions of *Mame* (with Ann Miller) and *Promises Promises* followed, but in 1973 Holiday's career took a new—yet still creative—turn after he visited the town of Hawley in the Pocono Mountains region of Pennsylvania. Impressed by this popular resort area and its beautiful Lake Wallenpaupack, he bought land and became a real estate developer.

"It was great to be in control of my own destiny," he recalled in *Superman on Broadway*. "The uncertainty of making a living in show business was beginning to affect me. After a while, I started my own business, Bob Holiday Homes. I found that I had a real knack for house design, and I found much personal satisfaction and happiness. I didn't miss the show business life, and felt that I was making a great fresh start."

Metropolis Bound
After nearly 30 years of building custom mountain retreats, Holiday Googled BOB HOLIDAY SUPERMAN while surfing the web one night and saw himself referenced on multiple sites. He also learned about the annual Superman Celebration in Metropolis, Illinois. One thing led to another, and he connected with Hollywood-based author, musician, pop-culture consultant, and Superman expert Chuck Harter. Soon they were working together on Holiday's biography *Superman on Broadway* and had arranged for the 1966 Man of Steel to be a 2003 Metropolis celebrity guest. Fellow celebrities would include the First Lady of Metropolis Noel Neill (Lois Lane in the Superman movie serials, 78 episodes of the

1950s television series, and Lois' mother in *Superman the Movie*), Yvonne Craig (the first woman to portray a DC Comics superhero—Batgirl—in the third season of ABC-TV's *Batman*, in 1967), and acclaimed DC Comics Superman artist Steve Rude.

Harter recruited Los Angeles-based technical consultant Steve McCracken to do layout and graphics on the book and to co-produce videos for Holiday's stage show. Harter and Holiday then invited me to join the team and assist McCracken in filming the documentary we later titled *Holiday in Metropolis*. I had met Harter through our mutual friend Jim Hambrick (owner of the Metropolis Super Museum) a few years earlier during a business trip to Los Angeles.

This invitation was exciting news for me; I grew up in New York City and clearly remembered the newspaper ads for *"It's a Bird...It's a Plane...It's Superman"* when I was twelve years old. Why I didn't ask my mother to take me to that show I'll never know. She was a regular theatregoer and midtown Manhattan was a half-hour subway ride from our Bronx neighborhood. Looking back, I think it was because I was besotted with *Batman* on television, and had the vague notion from the newspaper ads that the Broadway musical was somehow making fun of Superman. Of course, today it's clear that *Batman* was being played for laughs far more than *"It's a Bird...It's a Plane...It's Superman"* was. In any case, I'll always regret not seeing Bob flying high in that musical.

My Dinner With Bob
Bob Holiday and I had had several lengthy get-acquainted phone conversations prior to meeting for the first time at the Memphis International Airport on Wednesday June 11, 2003. I flew in from New York, and he from Scranton. Together we sat, talked, and waited to board Northwest Flight 3399 at 1:10pm to Paducah, Kentucky—closest airport to Metropolis, Illinois. Bob was now 71 (I'm 68 as I write this 20 years later), and I had only seen him previously in stills from his Broadway shows. It was clear, however, that he still had the kind of commanding presence necessary for the Broadway stage. Six-feet-four inches tall (he

beat me by an inch), with a deep baritone, Bob (as I now knew him) the homebuilder was still a star.

In the weeks leading up to the 2003 Superman Celebration my wife and I had obtained a few karaoke CD's Bob asked us to get for him at Colony Music in Times Square. Ironically, the store was just down the block on 52nd Street from what used to be the Alvin Theatre where Bob's Superman sang and flew in 1966. (Colony had a massive inventory, and was a reliable source for hard-to-find records before iTunes existed; it closed its doors in 2012 after 64 years in business when the Brill Building—the store's landlord—tripled the rent.) The karaoke CD's were songs Bob planned to sing on Friday night in the AmeriHost Inn Theatre, and included such classics as "The Birth of the Blues" and the jazz standard "All of Me." He also sang "If Ever I Would Leave You" from his *Camelot* days as Sir Lancelot.

After a short hop north flying above the Mississippi River, Bob and I arrived at our destination. Mindful of needing to capture ample "coverage" for our documentary, I videotaped Bob from behind as he exited the plane at Paducah Airport, and then asked him to re-board and exit again so I could shoot a reverse angle from outside as he again descended the mobile stairway to the tarmac. *Should cut-together nicely*, I thought.

John Stanton from the Metropolis Chamber of Commerce met us curbside at the airport and drove us to the AmeriHost Inn. I captured a few shots of passing road signs from the back seat along the way, filming over Bob's shoulder through the windshield (METROPOLIS BROOKPORT ½ MILE; THE MASSAC COUNTY CHAMBER OF COMMERCE WELCOMES YOU TO METROPOLIS HOME OF SUPERMAN).

After checking-in Bob and I found that Chuck Harter and Steve McCracken hadn't arrived from L.A. yet. We decided to have a late lunch at the nearby Harrah's Casino riverboat. It was a definite highlight of the weekend for me: just Bob and I, without distractions. Looking back, I wish I had tape-recorded our conversation. Bob had so many fascinating things to tell me. Here's the few I can remember:

• He sold football programs as a young boy at the Polo Grounds in Upper Manhattan after his parents divorced and he and his mother moved from Sea Gate, Brooklyn to Washington Heights. Bob's *modus operandi* was to hop on the downtown subway for a few stops with the first wave of departing spectators after the game, pick up their discarded programs, change trains, ride back uptown to the Polo Grounds, and then re-sell the programs to other spectators still leaving the stadium.

• He knew "a cute and zany little blonde girl" in the chorus of a tent revival of *Lady in the Dark* at the Westbury Music Fair in 1964. She surprised him one day when she said she was moving to Los Angeles to try to break into the movies. "She was such a tiny little thing, I feared for her safety, all alone in big bad Hollywood," Bob recalled. "But she was determined to become a star. Her name was Goldie Hawn."

• He idolized Sammy Davis, Jr., saying you had to see the man sing live on stage to realize what a phenomenal talent he was (a fact attested to by many). Bob said he always had Davis in mind when he sang.

• LIFE magazine had photographed Bob hanging from a flying harness in front of a large aerial backdrop projection of Times Square for the cover of its March 11, 1966 edition. Being on the cover of LIFE was the pinnacle of fame back then, and Bob looked forward to sharing that distinction with multiple Presidents, The Beatles, and James Bond 007 as the cover date neared. Then, at the last minute LIFE's editors substituted an image of *Batman*'s Adam West for the cover, due to the colossal popularity of that series, which had debuted on January 12. The photo of Bob was moved to the inside of the issue, one of several pictures illustrating the cover story, titled, "The Whole Country Goes Supermad." It was Bob's first brush with "capelash," but it wouldn't be his last.

• He and Jack Cassidy would improvise "little bits of business" on stage during each performance of *"It's a Bird...It's a Plane...It's Superman."*

Clark Kent had milk and cookies on his desk and would dunk them while other cast members were doing dialogue. At another point during the show when he'd fly off as Superman, Cassidy would hand him an envelope and say, "Hey, mail this for me, will ya?"

• He had to time his consumption of beverages carefully so as not to have to "go" during performances. The Superman suit took extra time to get in and out of.

• He was never offered to star in a new Superman television series in the late-1960s, despite what many have claimed on Internet posts.

• He auditioned for a Los Angeles production of *Promises Promises* at Burt Bacharach's house in the Hollywood Hills, and the famous songwriter was so impressed he hired him on the spot. Later, fellow *Promises Promises* actor Tony Roberts told Bob's ex-wife that Bob was "the most well-prepared actor he'd ever worked with."

• He invented one of the leading television game shows during the early 1970's (he wouldn't tell me which one), only to have his idea stolen from him. It's still on the air today. This and his still-vivid disappointment over not getting Mike Brady and a shot at breaking into Las Vegas headlining as the *Brady Bunch* daddy all prompted him to say, "I've had many disappointments, but that's true for most people…and that's life. Right now though I can't wait to meet the folks in Metropolis!"

Reporting From Metropolis
If one picture is worth 100,000 words, the video documentary *Holiday in Metropolis* must be good for a million. McCracken and I filmed it (wearing matching BOB HOLIDAY HOMES baseball caps) during the entire Celebration weekend using twin Panasonic AG-DVX100 MiniDV camcorders. The video captures the highlights of Bob's three days of autograph signings, fan interactions, the group Q&A session (with fellow celebrity guests Noel Neill and Yvonne Craig), and his nightclub act at the AmeriHost Inn Theatre. It also includes some random street interviews with fans, several of who provided poignant, fascinating, and

enlightening anecdotes of their reasons for attending the Celebration. Go to YouTube, type in "Holiday in Metropolis," and you should be able to find it easily. I hope you enjoy it. Steve McCracken did a superb job of turning our many hours of raw videocassette footage into a cohesive 54-minute story.

In addition to confirming my admiration and respect for the talents and people-skills of Bob Holiday, the weekend also afforded me the opportunity to converse with the lovely and gracious Noel Neill, whose portrayal of Lois Lane opposite *Adventures of Superman* star George Reeves was a daily television viewing ritual during my childhood. Ms. Neill was just as cordial and forthright in real life as she had been decades earlier as the spunky *Daily Planet* reporter. Former Batgirl Yvonne Craig was also a delight, as was her sister Meridel Carson. I learned that it was Meridel we actually saw in long-distance exterior shots of Batgirl riding her motorcycle in the *Batman* television series. Apparently the bike was built for style (complete with a lace fringe), but not safety. The show's producers didn't want to risk Yvonne getting injured if she fell off, so Meridel was her stand-in. This use of sibling look-alikes filmed from a distance is not uncommon in Hollywood.

Visiting Metropolis also enabled me to reconnect with Jim Hambrick, the world's greatest Superman collector and founder of The Super Museum (see Chapter Two). Jim and I had first met 20 years earlier on June 15, 1983 at The News Building in midtown Manhattan. He was there exhibiting part of his amazing collection in the building's landmark lobby, which appeared in a scene in *Superman: The Movie*. Just as no other city but New York could have portrayed Superman's Metropolis, no other newspaper but the *Daily News*—complete with its lobby's impressive 12-ft. diameter globe—could have played the role of the *Daily Planet*'s headquarters.

Jim was there on behalf of exercise equipment maker DP Gympac, whose products were featured in *Superman III*, which was premiering nationwide that week. DP (Diversified Products) hired Jim to create an exhibit titled "The Five Faces of Superman," spotlighting the character's theatrical cartoons, movie serials, *Adventures of Superman* television series, Saturday-morning cartoons, and Christopher Reeve movies. My wife had seen an announcement of the exhibit in that morning's *Daily News*, and I made a beeline for the lobby on the way to work. Meeting Jim and seeing part of his amazing collection was a memorable occasion and the start of a long friendship.

Fast-forward to 2003, and Jim's ever-growing collection now occupied an entire building in Metropolis. On Thursday morning he gave Bob a guided tour of The Super Museum, which included a special corner dedicated to *"It's a Bird...It's a Plane...It's Superman"* and its star. Bob was quite impressed with Jim's collection, which included an original 1966 *Playbill* for the show, photos of Bob in costume, and a painting depicting a scene from the musical. "Bob reminds me of Kirk," Jim later told me. "The way he carries himself with dignity. The mark of a very professional performer." *Kirk* was Kirk Alyn, Superman in the 1948 and 1950 movie serials, who had been managed by Jim during the later years of his career.

The Celebration weekend's big event was Bob's Friday-night command performance, in tuxedo, at the AmeriHost Inn Theatre. He told jokes, reminisced about his time as Superman, talked about his "brothers" (the other actors famous for that role, particularly George Reeves and Christopher Reeve), and sang "All of Me" and "If Ever I Would Leave You." That latter song lacked a karaoke disc but McCracken was able to masterfully separate the vocal and instrumental tracks on a *Camelot* original cast CD, which worked perfectly. A few months later I saw Lionel Ritchie basically do the same thing during a conference in Amsterdam. Technology is amazing.

Saturday was another busy day of filming Bob autographing 8 by 10 photos and copies of *Superman on Broadway*, kibitzing with attendees, and fielding questions during a Q&A with Noel, Yvonne, and Steve. The Midwest summer sun beat down hard on us all, but bottles of cold water and the giant tent provided by City National Bank saw us through.

Saturday night we all returned to the theatre for the charity auction. We filmed that too. It's all there in *Holiday in Metropolis*.

Revivals

Sunday morning, June 15, 2003 found us all in the waiting room of Barkley Regional Airport in Paducah for a flight to Memphis that would take everyone to their respective final destinations. I felt a bit sad that the event had come to an end. McCracken had all the MiniDV videocassettes we shot stuffed into his backpack, and I didn't envy him the task of editing it into a documentary when he got back to L.A. As noted above, he did a superb job.

As I sat with Bob he reiterated his satisfaction at having interacted with so many enthusiastic fans in Metropolis, and his enjoyment of being back in a tuxedo, on stage in front of an audience. I pulled my copy of *Superman on Broadway* out of my camera bag and asked him for one last Superman Celebration 2003 autograph. He wrote, "To Brian: Without your participation our success would not have been to the level it became. My fondest respect for your talents and humility. My thanks from the heart, you were always there! — Bob Holiday."

Fortunately, this would not be the last time I'd see Bob Holiday. Four years later there were two small revivals of *"It's a Bird...It's a Plane... It's Superman"* in Manhattan. Six years later, in 2013, a much larger and more elaborate revival (albeit without flying) was staged at the City Center Theatre on West 55th Street. Bob attended all three revivals, and so did I. These were great opportunities to reconnect with Bob and witness more of Superman's Broadway history as it happened. I reviewed each production for Bob's website, SupermanBobHoliday.com. The site had been created by Steve McCracken in 2003, and then passed along to a new admin, Toni VallesKey Collins, a few years later. Toni had seen the original 1966 Broadway production of *"It's a Bird...It's a Plane...It's Superman"* as a child. Impressed with Bob's performance ever since, she reached out to him decades later and became his close friend. Toni has done a wonderful job of adding fresh new content to

Bob's website ever since, including the reviews I wrote. Like me, Toni is committed to making people aware of Bob's rightful place in Superman's live-action history. I'll tell you more about this remarkable woman after the reviews, which I present here.

The first revival that I attended was on March 12, 2007 at The Opening Doors Theatre Company (ODTC) at the Duplex Cabaret Theatre in Greenwich Village. I had the honor of not only sitting with Bob and his daughter Kelly but also with Broadway's original Lois Lane Patricia Marand and her husband Irv Salem. My report follows.

March 12, 2007

On March 12, almost 41 years to the day that "It's a Bird...It's a Plane...It's Superman" premiered on Broadway, the original Lois and Clark of the 1966 musical that the New York Times called "The best musical of the season" reunited to attend a modest revival production by the Opening Doors Theatre Company (ODTC) at the Duplex Cabaret Theatre in Greenwich Village.

After being greeted by fans and well-wishers, Patricia Marand and Bob Holiday and the rest of the audience turned their attention to a tiny stage animated by a dozen fresh young faces with the kind of singing and acting skills you'd expect to see on Broadway, which— when you're in Manhattan as we were—is actually just a short walk from the ODTC. This tremendously fun-filled musical comedy was brought to life under the direction of Casey Burden and choreographer Rick Delancy.

Performed in a space barely large enough to hold 100 people (actors included), what the production lacked in size and stagecraft was made up for by the talent and enthusiasm of its well-directed cast. This was, after all, Off-Off Broadway, where spartan production values are the norm. What really mattered were energetic performances that provided just the right touch to this lighthearted musical comedy. Superman (played by the mesmerizingly confident Rob Ventre) didn't fly onstage. His costume was a Superman T-shirt and a pair of Clark Kent's dress slacks. Metropolis consisted of a small, black, canvas-backed stage. Musical accompaniment was a single piano nimbly played by Musical Director Steven Bednasz. But who misses elaborate sets and staging when you're having a rollicking, fast, funny, and totally engaging good time? The audience was too busy being entranced by the comic brilliance and singing voice of Sarah Lilley (Lois Lane), the lovably evil crooning of Andrew Cao (Daily Planet gossip columnist Max Mencken), the vampy delights of Suzanne Adams (Mencken's secretary Sydney), and the utterly hilarious Jason B. Schmidt (as the evil and hirsute villain Dr. Abner Sedgwick).

With songs by Broadway supermen Charles Strouse and Lee Adams (Bye Bye Birdie, Applause) and a book by the late David Newman and Robert Benton (co-authors of three of the Christopher Reeve Superman movies), it's still hard to believe that the original 1966 "It's a Bird..." didn't have as long a run onstage as Strouse's other comic-strip-inspired musical, Annie.

I digress. It's too bad this ODTC's revival was only three nights long. They should move the show to a larger venue and run it for at least a week. It's solid fun, through and through. "It's a Bird..." was one of the ODTC's "Closing Notice" concerts, which the program booklet describes as "Loving tributes to 'flop' shows or musicals that had criminally short runs yet fun scores of merit." "It's a Bird..." is often revived by local theater companies (most recently by the Musical Theater Guild at the Alex Theater, in Glendale CA). If such a revival comes to your town, by all means see it. Let's hope it's as good a production as the ODTC's was.

On a personal note, this reporter was honored to sit at Patricia Marand and Bob Holiday's table during the performance and enjoy their company and that of Mr. Holiday's lovely daughter Kelly and Ms. Marand's gracious husband Irv Salem. It was a great feeling to occasionally steal sidelong glances at Ms. Marand and Mr. Holiday during the show and see the smiles that this performance of "It's a Bird..." brought to their faces. Their presence at the revival was a delight to the actors and the audience alike. At one point during the show Bob leaned over to me and whispered, "You should have seen it on Broadway," and I realized what an incredible show it must have been on a full-size stage with million-dollar production values.

Patricia Marand and Bob Holiday made Superman history in 1966 with their acclaimed performances in "It's a Bird...It's a Plane...It's Superman," and they made a lasting impression on an audience yet again on March 12, 2007 with their visit to the show's revival. They continue to embody the beauty and gallantry, respectively, that the world has long associated with Lois and Superman. Thanks to them, the world renown of these great characters continues to inspire and provide a lasting sense of wonder.

June 16, 2007

Just three months later, I had the pleasure of seeing Bob again for another Manhattan revival of his show. This time it was uptown in the basement of the 59-story Citigroup skyscraper on 53rd Street. Patricia Marand and Irv Salem were vacationing in Spain, but my wife and daughter accompanied me this time, curious to meet the Superman I had been corresponding with. (The four of us had lunch after the show.) Also in attendance were Charles Strouse and Lee Adams! Here's that review.

Mufti is a word the dictionary defines as "civilian clothes." The York Theatre Company defines the term as "In street clothes without the usual trappings of a large production." Operating out of the 178-seat Theatre at St. Peter's Church (in the Citigroup Center in Manhattan's Midtown East neighborhood), "Musicals in Mufti" is the York Theatre Company's ongoing series of concert revival readings of under-appreciated Broadway musicals. Each show is presented by actors reading from the script, with practically no staging. The cast stands side-by-side in a row, behind music stands, reading their parts and facing the audience as they act and sing. It's not Broadway in terms of production pizzazz, but it is in terms of talent, with actors drawn from Broadway, off-Broadway, and recent films.

Lee Adams and Charles Strouse flank Bob Holiday at a June 2007 revival production.

From June 15th to 17th, the York Theatre Company's "Musicals in Mufti" series presented "It's a Bird...It's a Plane...It's Superman," and at the Saturday, June 16th matinee performance the role of Perry White was played by the show's world-famous composer Charles Strouse (Annie, Bye Bye Birdie, Applause). Members of the audience included Superman lyricist Lee Adams and the original Broadway Superman, Bob Holiday.

Presented in minimalist fashion as "reader's theatre," this production absorbed the audience's attention right from the start. Like a classic radio drama (complete with narration), this latest revival of the short-lived but much loved 1966 Hal Prince musical filled the mind's eye with vivid images of Metropolis, the Daily Planet newsroom, and Superman's never-ending battle for truth, justice, and his inability to express true love for Lois Lane. Giving life to this grand illusion—comprised in equal parts of endearing

Strouse/Adams songs and the late David Newman and Robert Benton's witty script—was a superb cast drawn from such shows as Wicked, Hairspray, Mama Mia, and other Broadway hits playing just a few blocks away. It was all directed to perfection by Stuart Ross, a Superman veteran who also directed the Goodspeed Opera House's elaborate 1991 production of the musical.

Chief among the acting talents were: Lea DeLaria as the hilariously evil Dr. Sedgwick (a woman this time around, and as maniacal as any mad scientist the stage or screen has ever presented); Jean Louisa Kelly as the poised, confident, yet conflicted Lois Lane (torn between unrequited love for the Man of Steel and the prospect of settling down with handsome scientist Jim Morgan [wonderfully portrayed by Stan Chandler]); David Rasche as the unscrupulous columnist Max Menken; Shoshana Bean as his long-suffering assistant Sydney; and Cheyenne Jackson as the square-jawed, utterly honest, strapping Superman. His "flying" consisted of an "Up, up, and away!" followed by a stationary pantomime of arms extended out, banking to and fro, and then lifting the binder holding his script and "flying" it away. Walking out of the spotlight with the utmost seriousness, holding his binder aloft as a child would a toy airplane in imaginary flight, Jackson's move was amusingly inventive and quite evocative of super-flight in the best Christopher Reeve fashion.

Every one of the principal characters had one or more signature songs, and each performer rendered them magnificently. In keeping with the modest staging, musical accompaniment consisted of music director Torquil Munro on piano and Larry Lelli on drums.

Two new songs, "Thanks to You" and (after the intermission) "Nuts to You," have been added to the show, both sung by the entire company. "Thanks to You" is (in the opinion of this reviewer) an improvement over the original show's number "It's Super Nice," which sounds dated to today's ears. Like that now-deleted ditty, "Thanks to You" is sung by Metropolis Institute of Technology students just before Superman's fall from grace. Other new material includes the character La Tete (played with a hilarious French accent by Michael Winther) and his Gallic band of evil "Cirque du Soleil rejects." This new band of ethnic bad guys replaces the original 1966 version's oriental stereotypes The Flying Lings and the equally objectionable 1975 ABC-TV version's thuggish Italian-American mobsters. Hopefully nobody will be offended this time around by funny Frenchmen.

"It's a Bird...It's a Plane...It's Superman" moved along at a brisk pace, culminating in its climactic scene of Superman shaking off Dr. Sedgwick's debilitating psychoanalysis and settling the bad guys' hash in short order. A new epilogue—written, according to director Ross, by the late David Newman for the 1991 Goodspeed production—has Lois again interested in Superman, but refusing his offer for a flight home. She opts to take a cab instead and replies "call me, we'll do lunch," indicating that Supes will have to finally make an effort to get to know Lois if their romance is to have a future. This is a nice contemporary twist on Lois' traditional role as perpetual damsel in distress. For the audience, the York Theatre Company's "Musicals in Mufti" production of "It's a Bird...It's a Plane...It's Superman" is a nice addition to their great series of staged concert performances of overlooked musicals—and a joy throughout.

Capping the show as the cast took their bows was Cheyenne Jackson's gracious call-out to Bob Holiday, which elicited further applause when Bob rose and waved at the audience. The show was followed by a Q&A between James Morgan, Producing Artistic Director of the York Theatre Company, and Charles Strouse, Lee Adams, Stuart Ross, Torquil Munro, and several members of the extremely talented cast.

Strouse recalled that securing DC Comics' permission to license its most famous character as a Broadway musical required producers Hal Prince and Ruth Mitchell to place the word Superman at the end of the title, as opposed to the beginning. Titling the show in such a way would, apparently, provide better protection for DC's trademark over time.

BRIAN MCKERNAN

Prompted by audience questions, Strouse confirmed the generally held view that the original show's run of only 129 performances was due to the societal craze triggered by the twice-weekly Batman TV series, which premiered just weeks before "It's a Bird...It's a Plane...It's Superman." The public incorrectly perceived the musical as a campy Batman-style send-up for kids. Matinees were added and packed with parents and children, but evening performances became sparsely attended. Confirming this was one of the many people who greeted Bob Holiday after the Q&A, a woman who stated she had taken her son to the 1966 production no fewer than six times!

Strouse raised the point that "It's a Bird...It's a Plane...It's Superman" was the first musical based on a comic-book character. Now that Spider-Man is headed for Broadway, he noted, perhaps it's time for Superman's big-budget return to the Great White Way. A split-second later Bob Holiday jokingly shouted, "Hey, Charles, do you think I have a shot at getting the part again?"

Another round of audience applause confirmed yet again that Broadway's original Superman will always be the standard against which all future musical superheroes are measured.

March 23, 2013

Six years after the York Theatre Company's production of *"It's a Bird... It's a Plane...It's Superman"* a larger and far more elaborate revival (albeit without flying) was staged at the City Center Theatre on West 55th Street. This was the last time I saw Bob, who attended the Saturday matinee performance with daughter Kelly and her husband. Mild-mannered reporter that I am, I started writing my review as soon as I returned home, and Toni posted it the next day. Here goes....

"This has been the Bob Holiday season here at Encores," noted Jack Viertel, the Artistic Director of the Encores! program at New York's City Center. "In January we also did Fiorello!" Viertel was referring to Holiday's 1959 Broadway debut in which he played the character of Neil, eager young assistant to New York City's Mayor La Guardia, in the 1959 Tony and Pulitzer Prize-winning Jerry Bock/Sheldon Harnick musical.

The occasion for Viertel's observation was a special "post-performance dialogue" that he moderated after the Saturday, March 23rd 2013 matinee performance at the City Center Theatre. More relevant to Viertel's remark, however, was that Bob also played the titular hero in the original 1966 production of "It's a Bird...It's a Plane...It's Superman," a show revived that very day just prior to Viertel's panel discussion. Holiday was in the audience for that rousing and delightful musical, which was one of the shows that Encores! chose for its 20th season of performing overlooked classics of the Broadway stage.

Brought to colorful, engaging life in just a few weeks by the incredibly talented artists of City Center, this revival of "It's a Bird...It's a Plane...It's Superman" provided audiences with what may well be the closest approximation yet to the original Broadway production. Although designated as a "concert production," the City Center's version was quite elaborate, and featured a full orchestra, brilliant direction, superb performances, inspired choreography, and innovative staging and lighting. The only scripts in evidence were those tossed by Superman at the villainous Flying Lings at the end of the show. Watching this new version, it was easy to understand why the March 30, 1966 review of the original production by New York Times critic Stanley Kauffmann included such comments as: "...it's fun...it would be enjoyable in any season...the whole show has been based on a witty point of view." This was all still true, and what a pleasant contrast the show was to the dark portrayals of comic book heroes that have come to haunt movie screens and even Broadway (i.e., Spider-Man: Turn Off the Dark) in recent years. This bright, colorful, optimistic show made you wish that Superman would turn the world back for us all by about 47 years, to when superheroes were colorful, uncomplicated characters and it was easy to tell the good guys from the bad.

Presented from March 20 to 24, City Center's Encores! revival of the 1966 Hal Prince musical "It's a Bird...It's a Plane...It's Superman" also did full justice to its catchy Charles Strouse-Lee Adams songs and clever Robert Benton-David Newman book. Unlike many regional revivals of this show over the years, City Center's version benefited from what was literally its Broadway-caliber talent, starting with director John Rando and extending throughout its cast, which included actors from such shows as Scandalous (Superman Edward Watts), Grease (Lois Lane Jenny Powers), Wicked (Alli Mauzey), Priscilla: Queen of the Desert (Will Swenson), Golden Child (James Saito), and many others. As legendary composer Charles Strouse noted later during the post-performance dialogue, "Where else can you find a cast as wonderful as this, except in Metropolis?"

Backed by the Encores! Orchestra (directed and conducted by Rob Berman), the singing of Powers and Mauzey, in particular, delivered the full lyrical impact of such Strouse-Adams compositions as "What I've Always Wanted" and "You've Got Possibilities." These and other numbers left no doubt that Powers and Mauzey were worthy heirs to the original production's female

Bob Holiday and *Superman* actor Edward Watts after the March 23, 2013 performance at New York's City Center Theatre.

leads: the gorgeous soprano Patricia Marand (Lois Lane) and the playful, jazzy Linda Lavin (Sydney). David Pittu's mad scientist Dr. Abner Sedgwick and Will Swenson's maniacal gossip columnist Max Mencken were also standout performances. And the actor upon whom so much depended—Edward Watts—was nothing short of spectacular in his dual role as both the awkward Clark Kent and courageously unpretentious Superman. Further empowering Watts' performance was costume consultant Paul Tazewell, who created one of the best-looking Superman costumes ever in terms of color and design, complete with an accurate and perfectly executed "S" symbol.

Then there was the show-within-a-show: the Flying Lings, a team of resentful Chinese acrobats who blame their unemployment on Superman's superior ability to amaze the public. Portrayed by Craig Henningsen, Suo Liu, Jason Ng, and Scott Webber—whose collective talents include spectacular abilities in martial arts, acrobatics, tumbling, and ballet—the Flying Lings performed a show-stopping sequence that including precision-choreographed pole-twirling, swordsmanship, and backflips. At a time when audiences nationwide are paying top dollar to see The Peking Acrobats touring company, the City Center's "It's a Bird...It's a Plane...It's Superman" gave audiences what could be almost considered as a "free preview" along with the show. Even more remarkable was director Rando's comment during the post-performance dialogue that several of the "Lings" had never been on stage before.

"I wanted them to be formidable opponents to Superman," Rando related. "When we called them in and first saw them perform, all we could say was 'Wow!' " This was the audience's reaction as well. Also, any lingering impression left by previous revivals of the Lings as offensive ethnic stereotypes was blown away by their kick-ass capabilities and determination in the City Center's rendering of the characters. If there was any stereotype in the show it was Pittu's Dr. Sedgwick as a quintessentially eccentric Oxford don, complete with the "Hogwarts" accent and old-school British mannerisms to go with it.

Joshua Bergasse's 1960's Hullabaloo-style go-go choreography, scenic consultant John Lee Beatty's brightly colored comic book cutout Metropolis skyline backdrop, lighting designer Ken Billington's bold use of bright primary colors on the background cyc to match the story's changing mood, and stage manager Tripp Phillips' efficient use of minimal set pieces wheeled in and out on casters all contributed to a fast-paced, totally enjoyable viewer experience that deftly conveyed the comic-book esthetic of the subject material.

As if this Encores! revival wasn't enjoyable enough already, Viertel's post-performance dialogue provided behind-the-scenes background details that enriched the experience. In addition to Viertel, Strouse, and Rando, participants in the session also included Strouse collaborator and lyricist Lee Adams, choreographer Bergasse, members of the cast, and other artists. During this 45-minute session, a number of fascinating details were revealed about the extreme dedication Encores! devotes to its productions. One was that they dug deep into the Tams-Witmark archives to find the original annotated sheet music arrangements for the 1966 production by legendary composer and jazz arranger Eddie Sauter, who orchestrated the show. The effort was well worth it, as the extra "zing" one hears on the Sony Broadway original 1966 cast CD was clearly audible during City Center's performance, and a delight to the ears.

"Sauter's sound was artistic and magnified it [our music]," Strouse recalled. "Sauter's sounds were streaked with excitement." Other comments about the score noted how the show's unique sound combined elements of 1950's/1960's Broadway, 1960's pop music, and jazz. As such, the score of "It's a Bird...It's a Plane...It's Superman" can be considered as an "evolutionary" link in the history of the American musical theatre.

Director Rando explained why the production elected to use a wooden cartoon cutout of Superman to depict his flights, as opposed to hanging actor Edward Watts from wires. "We didn't have the time to figure out how to fly our Superman," Rando explained. "And although it was a wacky idea, we all agreed the cutout actually worked." This reviewer agrees.

The inevitable question of the post-performance dialogue was, of course, why "It's a Bird...It's a Plane...It's Superman" only lasted 129 performances. Several reasons were suggested. A renown theatre historian on the panel cited the competition at that time, which included the original runs of some of the greatest musicals in the American musical theatre: Fiddler on the Roof, Man of La Mancha, Sweet Charity, and Mame. Charles Strouse also noted that the tone of the show may have been hard for 1966 audiences to understand; campy, but not as campy as the Batman TV series (which premiered 60 days earlier on ABC) and comical, but in a way that may be have been too subtle for the times. It was the latter reason, however, that Lee Adams cited, quoting the show's co-writer Robert Benton as attributing weak box office to "capelash"; the Batman TV craze sweeping the nation at the time had audiences assuming that "It's a Bird...It's a Plane...It's Superman" simply offered more of the same. Unfortunate but true.

A Q&A period concluded the post-performance dialogue session, and an intriguing detail was revealed in an answer to an audience member asking if this most enjoyable revival might be revived again in the near future by City Center Encores! The answer was that there were ongoing discussions about that very idea, as well as a possible TV version.

A fitting conclusion to the event came when Viertel, prompted by another audience question, asked original 1966 Broadway Superman Bob Holiday to stand up and take a bow. Wearing a sporty Superman jacket, Holiday waved to the audience, pointed toward his new friend Edward Watts, and acknowledged his great performance as the latest Superman. Judging by the number of autograph-seekers gathering around Holiday after the dialogue, however, it was clear that for many fans of the show, Bob Holiday will always be their favorite singing Man of Steel.

Superfriends

As I noted earlier, Toni VallesKey Collins had seen the original 1966 Broadway production of *"It's a Bird...It's a Plane...It's Superman"* as a child. "Bob Holiday was my friend for over a decade," Toni states on Bob's website. "I saw him as Superman when I was eleven years old, met him backstage (while watching him flirt with my beautiful mother), and spent 38 years singing along with the him on the *Superman* cast album. My oldest daughter once told me that I was perhaps the only person who could build a website for Bob because 'I was just old enough to have seen the Broadway show and just young enough to have majored in computer science.'"

"Bob really was my childhood hero," Toni continued. "I connected with him personally after he attended the 2003 Superman Celebration in Metropolis IL. Steve McCracken built Bob a web site, and I just happened to stumble upon it."

Toni's outreach to Bob resulted in a long-distance friendship via email and telephone, with Toni communicating from her home in California to Bob's in Pennsylvania. "Bob and I enjoyed occasionally writing to each other," Toni noted. "I asked whether he'd seen the biscuit commercial with the 'You've Got Possibilities' song. He wrote back, 'No. But the Pillsbury Dough Boy winked at me in the grocery store today.'" This friendship grew into weekly phone conversations between Toni and Bob, who found they shared many mutual interests. "It became my joy to call him every week," Toni recalled. "I rarely missed our weekly chats. I never had the chance as an adult to meet Bob Holiday in person. How is it that someone you met once at the age of eleven could become your true and dear friend so many years later?"

For my part I was frequently on eBay, searching for new Bob Holiday Superman images that I could pass along to Toni for Bob's website. One item that I knew to exist (having seen it on television decades earlier) was a long-lost television commercial Bob Holiday appeared in—as Superman—for Aqua-Velva aftershave. This was not a *Bob Hope Special*-style parody; this was color film footage of Bob, an official

Superman actor, photographed during the long live-action Superman gap between the last episode of the George Reeves *Adventures of Superman* television series in 1957 and the first Christopher Reeve Superman motion picture in 1978. I'm still not totally certain what year this commercial was filmed. It may have been in 1966; others claim it was in 1971. Bob couldn't remember, nor did he have a copy of it. It was on television decades before consumer VCRs became available. My inquiries to Aqua Velva went unanswered. Despite extensive Google and YouTube searches, I could never find this commercial. But then another strange Superman coincidence entered my life.

One morning at my barber's I began talking to a fellow customer who just happened to mention that he worked for the company that manufactures Aqua Velva. I also learned that the company is only six miles from my home. He provided a contact name, and after a few years of my periodic reminder emails, that contact eventually sent me a link to a video of the commercial, which was still in his company's archives. I'll never forget the excitement I felt when he emailed me the link, and when I phoned Bob that evening to tell him I was passing it along to him. I had Bob on the phone and could hear him watch it for the first time in decades, telling a grandchild sitting on his knee, "That's *me* in that video. That's *me!*"

This video is *now* on Bob's website, SupermanBobHoliday.com (as well as YouTube), along with other rare period Bob Holiday Superman film footage. This includes *The Story of Superman*, which is a mock-newsreel that was shown during Act 1, Scene 6 of the 1966 production of *"It's a Bird...It's a Plane...It's Superman"* and a rare 1966 episode of *I've Got a Secret* that Harter and McCracken located in which Bob teaches show host Steve Allen to fly from wires. Complementing Toni's website is a Facebook page I created, "Bob Holiday: Broadway's Superman." I hope you'll visit that as well.

More Coincidences

Thanks to Toni's website efforts, Bob Holiday steadily began to regain recognition as a former Superman, reclaiming his rightful place alongside radio's Bud Collyer, Kirk Alyn of the movie serials, and television's George Reeves. "Then one day Bob called me to say he needed to talk to me, that he didn't want me to read about this on the Internet," Toni recalled. "He was going in for open-heart surgery that week."

After his operation Bob relied on Toni even more. "When interviews became too taxing for his strength, we'd ask for written questions and Bob and I would work together on the answers, with me, again, typing them up," she explained. "When his computer broke down, I began reading his emails to him and typing back his answers to his fans."

"A few months before his death, Bob was rushed to the hospital," Toni continued. "I happened to call, and Bob's daughter Kelly let him know that 'Toni called this morning.' "'Aw,' he said, '*that's my buddy.*' It is a title I will cherish for the rest of my life. On Friday, January 27, 2017, the day Bob died, a small miracle occurred. Some people would say it was just a series of coincidences. But I say that when a slew of coincidences line up in a row, that's a miracle; someone upstairs is stirring the pot."

"I brought my purse and phone upstairs Thursday night, which I almost never do. I had my phone on 'ring,' not 'silent'; uncommon on a Friday. I was standing by my purse when Kelly texted, or I never would have heard it. The text said that Bob was strong enough for a phone call, which hadn't been the case for days. I had met some commitments a day early, so I was free to stay home and call Bob. And so on Friday, January 27, 2017, I got one last phone call with Bob Holiday. He was too weak to speak, so I sang to him a song from the show, I thanked him for years of friendship, and I said, 'You're going on a long journey, Bob, and the Lord will be there with you. I hope you'll accept His welcome when you meet Him.' "

After Bob died, his daughter Kelly asked Toni to continue building Bob's website. She is honored to continue building an archive for this tremendous actor.

Postscript

Christopher Reeve described himself as a "temporary custodian" of Superman in his 1998 autobiography *Still Me*. Noting that, Bob Holiday stated, "I was very proud to 'take care' of Superman in the 1960's. Playing the part was great fun, and I loved it. I still hear from fans today, and it's wonderful. Over and over, someone will find me, get in touch, and let me know how much they loved the show (and even me personally). You can't imagine how much that meant to me 40 years later."

Chapter Twelve

Superman at 75

"I was really interested about Superman and religion," stated biographer Larry Tye as he stood on the stage of the Leo and Julia Forchheimer Auditorium at the Center for Jewish History, in New York, on the afternoon of Sunday, January 27, 2013. Speaking to a packed house of more than 250 eager attendees (more than a few of whom had bright blue of Superman T-shirts visible at the neckline of their layered winter attire), Tye was explaining how a serious reporter such as he had decided to write *Superman: The High-Flying History of America's Most Enduring Hero* (Random House, 2012).

Tye began by describing his visit to the annual Metropolis, Illinois Superman Celebration, and the tumultuous welcome he witnessed for original Lois Lane actor Noel Neill. His visit was part of his book research, which led him to observe that, "Superman was like a religion for so many people that I wanted to understand what religion Superman himself was."

Convinced that writing a book about Superman would be a serious endeavor ("Understanding America's embrace of heroes says something about who we as Americans are," Tye noted), the author of five previous works of nonfiction undertook the task. Noting that Superman was *the* longest-lived hero of the last century, he added, "A few of the things that I found out about Superman…were a little bit of a surprise to me." Some of those things included Superman's role as a bond salesman in World War II, how his comic book editors kept him out of that conflict (he flunked an eye test by accidentally reading a chart in the next room with

DC and Marvel Comics writer Jim Shooter; moderator Larry Tye (standing); Sam Norich of the Forward Association; Nicky Wheeler-Nicholson Brown (granddaughter of Malcom Wheeler-Nicholson, founder of the company that became DC Comics); and former DC publisher and president Jenette Kahn.

his x-ray vision), the use of his radio program to undermine the KKK, and—of greatest significance—the fact that Superman was born out of the anguish felt by 17-year-old Joseph Siegel when his father suffered a fatal heart attack following a robbery at his Cleveland clothing store in 1932.

"So next time you look at a Superman movie or a comic book…or any kind of Superman story," Tye continued, "I want you to think not about some superhero story that somebody devised; I want you to think about a little bullied boy who was looking for a way to fight back against the world that seemed unfair. And I think that Jerry Siegel felt that if we were all smart enough and looked at this little boy...we would see inside of him the true Superman."

The Chosen

"The Center for Jewish History may seem like a curious place for a discussion and celebration about Superman, but in reality we are the perfect place," said Judith Siegel, the Center's director of academic and public programs. She spoke prior to introducing Tye, adding, "The Center for Jewish History is a consortium of five partner organizations. Together the collective archives of those partners number 100 million documents, films, music, historical records, memoirs, and much more."

Comprising the largest repository of Jewish history in the United States, the Center also serves as a centralized location for scholarly research, events, and exhibitions. On this particular day the Center's presentation topic was Superman, a character any ethnicity would be proud to call its own. Author Larry Tye spoke at length and was later joined onstage by a panel consisting of: former DC Comics president Jenette Kahn; comics writer, editor, and publisher Jim Shooter; Nicky Wheeler-Nicholson Brown, granddaughter of Malcolm Wheeler-Nicholson, who founded the company that became DC Comics; and Sam Norich, publisher of *The Jewish Daily Forward*.

"Every faith on this planet has claimed Superman as theirs," Tye explained during his introduction. "Christians say...the story of Superman is the story of Christ. If you were to go home after today's presentation and Google 'Buddhism and Superman' there would be entire treatises that had been written on the Zen of Superman. Who could be a more Zen-like character? Atheists and agnostics say 'Who needs religion, who needs God? We've got this character, this superhero who knows instinctively the difference between right and wrong and who behaves like we all ought to behave...he's the perfect secular messiah. What do we need religion for?'"

"So lots of people claim him, but I'm here today," Tye said—pausing briefly to unbutton his shirt to reveal a bright-blue T-shirt underneath with the familiar Superman "S" shield bordered by a red-and-yellow Star of David—"in this wonderful Center for Jewish History...to say that Superman is in fact one of the Chosen People."

The Evidence
"I want to share with you that there are lots of people over the years, including one of the people in our audience today, who've been piecing together wonderful lessons of Superman's Jewish roots, " Tye continued. "And I want to share with you just a couple of my more convincing pieces of evidence.

"Here is the story I want you to think about. There were parents who were worried about the destruction of their world, and to save their first-born son, their only child, they float him out, let's say, into outer space and he is discovered in the middle of the most middle-American part of America. He's discovered in the Midwest by two of the most extraordinary gentiles, named John and Martha Kent. John and Martha raised their child and realized over time that they had a really extraordinary child who's got some amazing powers. And that's...the story of Moses and Genesis."

"Even more timely, given what was going on in the lives of Jerry Siegel and Joe Shuster, is the story of the world that both of their parents left behind in Eastern Europe that was being destroyed," Tye continued. "And one of the things that were saved during the Holocaust...was the effort to save a small number of children that was called *Kindertransports*. And I think that Superman's escape from the Planet Krypton is a modern-day version of the *Kindertransport*."

Another compelling bit of evidence for Superman's Jewishness that Tye shared was the Man of Steel's family name. "We all know the name of Superman's father on the planet Krypton: *Jor-El*," Tye noted. "And Superman was *Kal-El*. In the Hebrew, you know what *El* means: *God*. And what is *Kal*? *Voice* or *vessel*. So maybe it was an accident that Jerry Siegel gave us the character who came to earth with a name that translates into 'the voice or vessel of God,' but I don't think so. What

Jerry told us in his memoir was, he never told us about Jewish roots, but gave us a little hint. He said, 'I write about what I know about.' And growing up in Glenville, Ohio, a neighborhood of Cleveland that was 70 percent Jewish, he knew about a world that was Jewish."

"The next big hit that Jerry tried to make in the comic book world was a character named Funnyman," Tye continued. "Funnyman, we all know, didn't go very far. Nobody tells me he knows who Funnyman is. But one thing you have to know about Funnyman, Jerry's next big strike, was a character who looked like Danny Kaye and who was overtly Jewish. And I think Jerry was not quite secure enough to give us Superman that's an overtly Jewish hero, but his next big-time 'Superman' was going to come out of whatever closet he was in. So Funnyman was a Jewish character."

"The last piece of evidence is my favorite, which is that any name that ends in the word *m-a-n* is one of two things: It's either a superhero or a Jew. Or in this case, it's both. So next time you look at a word spelled *Superman*, I want you not to think of it as Super-man, it is—" Tye quipped, pronouncing the word like a last name such as *Goldman* or *Kaufman*— "*Soopermun*."

Heroic Core
"What I would like to do is, I would like to take you back to where I started," Tye told the enthusiastic audience, which responded to his statements with frequent applause. "Where I started was, it was a serious purpose to write this book. And the purpose was to figure out why Superman has survived to the point where we can be celebrating today the first 75th birthday party for Superman. Why has he survived this long? What was the key to his survival? And to me it was two quite simple things."

"One was…that over the years Superman did what any character—what any hero to maintain his or her relevance had to do—which is evolve. That when Superman first came to us in 1938, America was mired in a Great Depression and what we needed was a character who was a lot like

FDR: a butt-kicking, New Deal liberal. And that's what Superman was. He was out there chasing wife-beaters and slumlords. No question about who he was voting for and what his politics were. He wore it on his arm, on his sleeve, and everywhere else.

"In the Forties when we needed somebody to give us the inspiration to go to war and to stay and safeguard the home front, Superman did that," Tye continued. "In the Fifties, the great American enemy or perceived enemy was red and Superman was out there tracking down the Red Menace. So part of Superman's success, 50 percent of it was that he evolved. He changed with the times and became the character that was perpetually relevant. An even more important reason of why he survived this long is exactly the opposite. It's because of what hasn't changed in Superman. At his core—and thankfully the handlers of DC and Warner Brothers and other places recognized this over the years—at his core what Superman is all about is a sense of righteousness, a sense of right and wrong."

"I think, personally—and this is my bias, and my microphone may go off because I hear that the AV guy's a big Batman fan—I think the world has enough dark heroes like Batman," Tye stated. "We certainly have enough fraught and anxious heroes like Spider-Man. What I think we need…[is] a hero, particularly in tough times like we're going through right now, who knows the difference between right and wrong. And you can call that old-fashioned and clunky, but it's also reassuring and familiar. And I think it's why Superman came before Batman and Spider-Man and, God willing, will survive all the superheroes who are out there."

Super Mensch
After introducing a friend who described how his father once served as a Superman model for artist Joe Shuster, Larry Tye was joined onstage by the Superman at 75 panelists. The group discussion began with Tye asking former DC Comics president Jenette Kahn what she thought made Superman special.

"When you were talking about the question of whether Superman is Jewish, in that context I would say he's a Super Mensch," Kahn replied. "That's really what he is. That is what I think has made him so important in our culture, is that he represents our best selves. He is what we aspire to. He shows us that we can have compassion, we can have ethics, that we can care about the person next to us. A person we don't even know, a total stranger."

"And he's had this code, the essence of Superman, that as Larry referred to, Superman always has to change," Kahn continued. "But we were always true to the core of Superman, to his Midwestern upbringing that came from Ma and Pa Kent that came also from his odyssey and his story, that he always had a sense of responsibility. He's very much the sage Hillel's saying, 'If I am not for myself, who am I? If I am for myself alone, what am I? If not now, when?' This is really the core of Superman, and the fact that he wants to be human, he wants to live among us, and enjoy the pleasures that we have as humans and the torments that we have as humans. And so we identify with Clark Kent and aspire to be Superman."

"I just think he's the greatest hero in the world," asserted comics writer, editor, and publisher Jim Shooter to wild applause after Tye asked him what he thought was "right or special about the guy."

"I remember a lot of things that [veteran Superman editor] Mort Weisinger had taught me. And Mort was a tough teacher, but he taught me a lot. The guy knew everything. And Julie Schwartz [veteran Superman editor who succeeded Weisinger], he was a hard case, too. One thing that they said that I agreed with, and Jenette has pointed out that the characters change and evolve and so forth...basically, an important thing to keep the same was the fact that he was *good*. There's no other way to say it. He's a *good* man. Whatever his concerns are for the moment or whatever trials and tribulations or pain you're putting him through, the fact is I think it's that good core, that good spirit that appeals to all of us. And packs [movie] houses."

"Julie said he was the one person that absolute power could absolutely not corrupt," Kahn added.

"Absolutely!" Shooter agreed. "Weisinger didn't say it as concisely as Julie did, but when I worked for Julie he would tell me how he wanted me to write Superman. He said, 'Get this straight: He doesn't lie, he doesn't make mistakes, he doesn't lose. He might be misled for a while, but he'll always figure it out. He's a good guy! Anything else?' I thought that was great. It was all about the honor of the character and the goodness of the character. I really think that 75 years later that's why he's still here. Because more or less that's been maintained."

Jewish Daily Forward publisher Sam Norich was then asked what he thought about how Superman "speaks" to Jewish audiences. "I had a lot to say until I came here," he joked, provoking laughter from the audience. "In the late Thirties Jews in America were in the crosshairs. American Jews felt like the bullied kid on the school play yard. What could they do? What could they do against Hitler's juggernaut? And their families in Europe were the ones who were really threatened. They needed something that could somehow stand up, at least in their youthful imaginations, against this. It was important that this something not identify himself as a Jew. This was a time in which Jews had to 'pass.' They shouldn't stand out too much. It helped if you were tall and you could take care of yourself." If you were like Superman, in other words.

"I got a lot of coaching at the top of their lungs from Mort Weisinger and Julie Schwartz," Shooter confided. "And among the things that each of them said repeatedly—and this ties into what was said at the beginning about how every religious group kind of finds a way to claim Superman —they wanted us to deliberately go out of our way *not* to exclude anyone. They said, 'Let everybody have their metaphorical occasion with Superman.' They were also sensitive to the audience in many ways. They didn't want to exclude people. I'm not saying that they didn't do— especially Julie—some stories that were topical and meaningful and so forth. But they really didn't want to nail it down. They wanted to leave it open to your interpretation."

"The most convincing evidence of Superman as a Christian was in the 1978 Christopher Reeve movie, particularly when Jor-El was played by the Godfather—Marlon Brando," Tye added.

Super Origins

"When we hear about Superman history we all think it began with Harry Donenfeld and Jack Liebowitz," Tye stated, referencing the entrepreneurial early owners of DC Comics. Tye directed his question at Nicky Wheeler-Nicholson Brown, whose grandfather, Major Malcolm Wheeler-Nicholson, founded the company in 1934 as National Allied Publications before ceding control to Donenfeld three years later. "Can you give us an inkling of what the real story was?"

"For our family this connection to Superman has always been a very powerful mythology," she replied, adding that she doesn't really consider herself a "comic industry insider."

"I became very interested in it about 13-14 years ago and started researching my grandfather, Major Malcolm Wheeler-Nicholson and his connection to DC Comics and whether he actually did start DC Comics itself. He and Jack Liebowitz were the two main owners of DC and he also started the company that was prior to that [National Allied Publications], which brought out *More Fun* and *New Fun*."

"Basically, the comic book mythology is that he did this because it didn't cost him money. Well…in our family just because it doesn't cost a lot of money doesn't have anything to do with it. It has to do with the creativity and the vision and the idea. Our grandfather was really interested in this popular cultural forum. He started using comic strips back in 1925, 1926, and 1927 to tell graphic stories of novels by Émile Zola, Edgar Allan Poe, and Robert Louis Stevenson—*Treasure Island*. So he had these ideas long before he got involved with the comic books themselves."

"I interviewed my aunt and my father, who are all now deceased," Wheeler-Nicholson Brown continued. "Our uncle is still living. They generally all told pretty much the same story that when he [Major Wheeler-Nicholson] saw the original drawing of Superman he *immediately* knew that this was *huge* and that it was really important. And Jerry Siegel himself said that without my grandfather they never would have made it into print because he hired them for his new comic books and they started doing Slam Bradley, Federal Men, Spy, and Calling All Cars. He knew right then and there that it was important, it had archetypal resonance. And he wanted to bring it out."

"Can I just tell a personal story?" Wheeler-Nicholson Brown asked. "When I was a little girl watching George Reeves on the television, I had a boyfriend whose name was Brad; we were about five. We would watch George Reeves and then we would pin a towel with safety pins to our t-shirts and then jump off the picnic table and fly. So it's not just little boys who want to fly, it's little girls, too. I was always Super*girl* and he was always Super*man*. One day I said, 'Why do *you* always get to be Superman? *I* should be Superman!' We had a little talk about it and finally he agreed that I could be Superman when he heard my statement that ended the discussion: *And my grandfather invented him!* I didn't have a clue, but I *knew* that my grandfather had *something* to do with Superman!"

The Man in the Mirror
An audience member then asked the crucial question: "Does Superman put his glasses *on* as a disguise or take them *off* as a disguise? Which one is the character? Which one is the disguise?"

"Jules Feiffer was the first person to answer that question for me in his book *The Great Comic Book Heroes*," replied Shooter. "He said that Superman doesn't have to have the Batmobile, the bat-suit, any of that stuff; he's *always* Superman. And so the disguise is when he puts the glasses *on*. And that's unique among heroes. I think that's another reason why people relate to him because nobody wants to have to put on their bat-suit to go out and beat up the bullies."

"He never puts on a mask, and that always makes him accessible," Kahn agreed. "The mask is the glasses. But as a hero, he always shows his face to us."

"That's what Jerry [Siegel] told us in his memoir when he tried to figure out what Clark Kent was like as a character," Tye added. "Clark Kent was *him*. And if people would look inside him they'd see there really was a Superman there. And Joe [Shuster] actually said that when he was looking for a model for how to draw Superman, he would look in a mirror. Now, *that* was one more piece of evidence that Joe *was* nearsighted."

Universal Appeal

"Superman is everywhere around the world, and people find ways to identify with him," Shooter noted. He then referenced the fact that he began sending his own Superman stories to DC Comics in 1965, when he was 13 years old. Editor Weisinger was so impressed with the stories that he began publishing them the following year. Shooter's parents appreciated the extra income.

"I had a friend whose father went on business to Dutch Surinam in the Sixties and he comes home with comic books. He said, 'I've got you a comic book; too bad you can't read it.' And I said, "That's okay, *I wrote it*." Someone came back from Viet Nam with a pile of comic books, and I wrote those too. Superman is all over the world. And the goodness of Superman really translates everywhere."

"We've always said that he's a citizen of every country in the world," Kahn agreed. "We actually did landmine comics at DC, for landmine awareness for kids in Bosnia and Croatia and Nicaragua and Costa Rica. And we started to get some blowback from the idea of Superman starring in comics. We actually suggested that we could do local heroes based on the images and the cultures of countries where we were going. And we were getting from *informaciones* and different factions that 'Superman was an imperialist capitalist tool.'"

"But when our partners on these comics—the State Department, and the U.N., and the Department of Defense—odd bedfellows, but when they did testing, all the kids everywhere wanted Superman. Because, again, it's what Superman stood for. He wasn't a *local* hero, he was this larger-than-life hero who meant so much to them. And in fact when we went to Mozambique—and we very much wanted in every country where we went to make sure that the landscape and the homes, everything reflected back to the culture that was there—I asked the people who were going from the Department of Defense would they please take disposable cameras and give them to the kids so they could photograph their own environment. And they were like 'Oh, that's a good idea, but how will we ever get these cameras back?' I said, not to worry, we gave them all Superman t-shirts. We got every camera back."

Reinforcing the idea of Superman's universal appeal was an audience member who pointed out that the very first published Superman adventure, in the 1938 *Action Comics* issue number one, included a story about him rescuing a woman being beaten by her husband. "In the same issue he stops an arms trader," Norich added. "No job too small, no job too big," Shooter commented.

"Jim is absolutely right about 'No job too small, no job too big,'" Kahn agreed. "If Superman didn't do the small jobs, he wouldn't have the common touch. Even in the great first Superman movie he rescues a kitten from a tree. And you always need that part, you need the *grounded* part of Superman that shows that he *cares* about the ordinary event that means so much on a personal basis to the woman who's being beaten or the girl whose lost her cat. Without that, Superman would be a little too grandiose. The fact that he has time for all of us is important."

"Let me tell you how important Superman was to us," Shooter added, referencing his years as editor-in-chief at DC competitor Marvel Comics. "When *Superman: The Movie* came out in 1978 I took the *whole* office to the first morning show, because I knew we could get into that one. I made them all watch it, and I didn't have to force them too much. And then when I came back Stan Lee called me into his office and he yelled at me, saying, 'Why didn't you invite *me?*' "

Fond Memory

As the two-hour Superman at 75 event drew to a close and attendees were awash in Superman-love and looking forward to the very large Superman birthday cake in the lobby of the Center for Jewish History, one last audience member stood to speak. His name was Steve Iger, who also happened to be a grandson of DC Comics co-founder Harry Donenfeld.

"Harry gave a tremendous amount of money to Jewish causes," Iger reminded. "He was a founder of Einstein Medical College. Jack Liebowitz went on to become president of Long Island Jewish Hospital. They were very generous people."

Iger then related the following story about his feelings for one particular Superman.

"Some of you look like you would remember Palisades Park. In 1955, there was Superman at Palisades Park Day. George Reeves comes out on stage, the middle of the summer, the hottest day of the year, as Clark Kent in his suit and glasses. Then he runs off stage, comes back as Superman, and the crowd goes wild. This is the one of the biggest crowds ever at Palisades Park. And afterwards Superman autographs pictures of himself. I was a little *pisher* of seven years old, and I had a stack of pictures I'm handing to George Reeves and the poor man was *shvitzing—that* suit was *wool*! Afterwards we went into the executive offices and my grandfather, Harry Donenfeld, knocked on George Reeves' dressing room door.

"'Who *is* it?' [Iger's tone of voice indicated that Reeves sounded annoyed.]

"'It's your *boss*!' [Donenfeld answered in a commanding tone.]

"'*Hi*, Harry.' [Reeves responded, suddenly very cordial.]

"And George Reeves came out and took a picture with his [Harry's] five grandchildren. His arms were out to *there*. It was like his arms were seven feet long. And *that's* the way we'd always feel about George Reeves."

Credit: Louis Koza

Chapter Thirteen

Celebration 2014: Reeves, Siegel, and Shuster

"Terrorist drones…a dynamite vest…an out-of-control nuclear reactor… computer crime…deadly asteroids. This is the stuff of modern newspaper headlines. These are also plotlines from a television series that ceased production nearly 60 years ago but continues to enthrall viewers, *and* is the reason we're all gathered here today. That series is *The Adventures of Superman*."

I spoke these words before a group of about 100 at a luncheon at the Beverly Garland Hotel in North Hollywood on the afternoon of August 16, 2014. The occasion was Super Celebration 2014, an event organized by Jim Nolt to mark the 100th anniversary of the birth year of George Reeves, Jerry Siegel, and Joe Shuster.

I was one of a dozen speakers, who also included: 86-year-old Jack Larson, Jimmy Olsen from *The Adventures of Superman* television series; Jerry Siegel's daughter Laura Siegel Larson; Ruta Lee and Beverly Washburn, both of whom appeared in episodes of the series; *Deadwood* actor and Reeves biographer Jim Beaver; Paul Bernbaum, screenwriter of *Hollywoodland*, the 2006 movie about Reeves' last days; Stephanie Shayne, daughter of Inspector Henderson actor Robert Shayne; Alejandro Vacio (via video), son of actor and Reeves pal Natividad Vacio; veteran stuntman Gene LeBell; Edward Lozzi, PR executive and friend of Reeves' inamorata Toni Mannix; and Bruce Dettman and Larry Ward, who relayed greetings from Lois Lanes Phyllis Coates and Noel Neill, respectively.

All a Wonder

Earlier that day our group of 100 or so George Reeves/*Adventures of Superman* fans had gathered at 5400 Wilbur Avenue in Tarzana to dedicate a plaque commemorating the location filming of an episode of that television series. Fellow fan Armand Vaquer had arranged for the plaque's engraving and secured permission from the site's property owner to install it. The plaque read:

ADVENTURES OF SUPERMAN.
Production years: 1951-1957. Producers: Robert Maxwell/Bernard Luber and Whitney Ellsworth.

Episode #29 "The Man Who Could Read Minds." Script by Roy Hamilton. Directed by Tommy Carr.

A portion of this episode was filmed in June, 1953 at 5400 Wilbur Avenue, Tarzana CA, and is the only location scene to feature all five main characters: Editor Perry White – John Hamilton; Reporter Lois Lane – Noel Neill (who replaced Phyllis Coates after the first season); Cub Reporter Jimmy Olsen – Jack Larson; Inspector Wm. J. Henderson – Robert Shayne; and Reporter Clark Kent/Superman – George Reeves.

A police stakeout scene was filmed at this location and a fight scene between Jimmy Olsen and the phantom burglar were filmed on Wilbur Ave. Additional chase scenes were filmed on Linnett Street.

Dedication of this plaque, provided by fans of the "Adventures of Superman," was held on August 16, 2014 to commemorate the 100th birthdays of George Reeves and Superman creators Jerry Siegel and Joe Shuster and over sixty years of the "Adventures of Superman."

Jack Larson arrived by limo and began the dedication by describing the television industry when *The Adventures of Superman* was in production. He took us all back to 1950:

"It's wonderful and astounding to see all of you who loved *The Adventures of Superman*," he began. "When we started it no one knew what we were doing. In 1950 most of the studios closed down with the rise of television, but it was *live* television. It was Milton Berle and such, *The Texaco Star Theatre* that changed everything, the whole exhibition

Credit: Steve Friedman

Jack Larson; fan Steven Kirk; Jacqueline Hamilton (granddaughter of "Perry White" actor John R. Hamilton); actress Beverly Washburn (child actress in *Superman and the Mole Men*); Adventures Continue president/event organizer Jim Nolt; Adventures Continue associate/monument supervisor Armand Vaquer. Kneeling: Stephanie Shayne (daughter of "Inspector Henderson" actor Robert Shayne) and Laura Siegel Larson (daughter of Superman writer/co-creator Jerry Siegel).

plans of the motion picture industry. At that point they realized there was a new challenge to the movie studios. We didn't know what television was. There had been no filmed television. At that time there was live television."

"I was suddenly offered to play Jimmy in *The Adventures of Superman*. I didn't know *what* it would be. I had never seen the serial. I was a *big* reader of the comic book *Superman*. I had the first editions for ten cents, which my mother threw away. Bob Maxwell, who was producing it, wanted to talk to me, and I went to the studio, and they said 'We want you to play Jimmy Olsen on 26 shows. And Jimmy wasn't in the comic books. So I didn't know what the heck they were talking about, but I did want to pick up the work, and go to New York, where there was a lot of live television and theater. So they said, 'We need you to make up your mind.' They were gonna shoot *Superman and the Mole-Men*, which Jimmy wasn't in, and *then* they were going to shoot 26 shows. So I said I have to think about it. I don't know anything about it. And I went to Venice Beach, down the street from where we were, and surfed for a bit, got a lot of tar on me I remember, and I thought *Well, why not?* I want to work, I wanted television, but I don't know what filmed television's going to be, so I came back and said I'd do Jimmy — *thank God!*"

"When I first became aware that Superman was an extraordinary event was when it went on the air. I was in New York, I took the money I made from the first 26, I went to New York, and took a little basement apartment around the corner from Madison and 82nd Street, and I used to walk and get breakfast at a ham-and-egg place on Madison Avenue. And I'd done live television, some films, and no one cared about me, and then *Superman* went on the air…and there were two things happened to me. When I'd go on Madison Avenue or anywhere, or try to take the subway…everybody would say, 'Hey Jimmy! Where's your pal with the cape?' Or the big one they'd say is 'Don't call me *chief!*' And that's the line that I'm best remembered for."

"It's all a wonder, "Larson concluded. "None of us would have known the show would be so beloved and out on DVD, and everyone sees it."

All the Marbles

Returning to the Beverly Garland that afternoon, the luncheon commenced with Nolt as master of ceremonies. Audience members included: John Hamilton Jr., son of Perry White actor John R. Hamilton; Gregory Moffett, who appeared as a boy in the 1956 *Adventures of Superman* episode "The Stolen Elephant"; John Rockwell, star of the unsold 1961 *Adventures of Superboy* television film pilot; Toni VallesKey Collins, admin of 1966 Broadway Superman Bob Holiday's website; *Superman: Serial to Cereal* author Gary Grossman; and three folks who came all the way from Australia. Incidentally, the hotel—now known as The Garland—was named after veteran actor Beverly Garland (1926-2008), whose many roles included Lois Lane's mother Ellen in six episodes of *Lois & Clark: The New Adventures of Superman*. Each guest received a commemorative coin designed by artist Randy Garrett.

It was quite an honor for me to be asked to say a few words, considering that the other speakers were entertainment industry veterans that included people who had known George Reeves personally. I did my best, and after citing how remarkably contemporary many of *The Adventures of Superman* plotlines were to today's world, I continued.

"The scripts for this series were given life by the talents of so many creative people, especially George Reeves, who—as Superman—saved the day in every episode before retreating into the secret identity of mild-mannered Clark Kent. *The Adventures of Superman* appealed to the Clark Kent in all of us, and was way ahead of its time, but—then again—wasn't Jerry Siegel and Joe Shuster's world-famous creation also known as 'The Man of Tomorrow?' "

"Jim Nolt has asked me to say a few words about Siegel and Shuster, without whom none of us would be here right now."

"My name is Brian McKernan; like all of you, I've been a fan of *The Adventures of Superman*—and its star, George Reeves—since childhood, but that's about it for my qualifications to be standing here. Many other people are far more qualified than I to talk about the two young visionaries who gave the world its most famous fictional character. But maybe the reason Jim asked me to do this is because I spent 25 years in New York magazine publishing. And if I learned one thing during that time it's that the guys who own those companies 'hold all the marbles.' You can put your heart and soul into your editorial efforts, but you'll always be just an employee. I was never employed by DC Superman Comics, but I'd always heard that it was a tough place to work."

"Siegel and Shuster knew that bitter truth far better than anyone; their story is thoroughly explored in excellent books by Brad Ricca and Larry Tye. I recommend them both. We all know the basics of the Siegel and Shuster story, which was not a happy one for them or their families. But, if I may dare to say this, there is quite an 'upside' to their story as well."

"Siegel and Shuster's Superman inspired a nation during the darkest days of World War II and during the long Cold War. Superman's radio series introduced young minds to racial and religious tolerance. Superman comics taught many of us to read, and *The Adventures of Superman* awakened an entire generation's sense of wonder, gently teaching us right from wrong, and even making guns impotent as they were crushed in George Reeves' powerful hands. Years later, Christopher Reeve made us all believe once again that a man could fly, both onscreen and in real life under awful circumstances."

"The show was the brainchild of the men who employed George Reeves and—a decade before that—Siegel and Shuster: DC Comics owners Harry Donenfeld and Jack Liebowitz. Those guys 'held all the marbles.' They owned the printing presses, employed the writers and artists (who they could fire at will), they controlled distribution, collected all the shiny dimes paid for the comic books they printed, and they eventually sold DC in the late Sixties to what would become Time Warner for a lot of money."

"Superman Inc. was big business, as Siegel and Shuster knew all too well. And although the past can't be changed, the riches generated by Siegel and Shuster's brilliant creation were not just monetary ones. They live on: in the camaraderie felt in this room, in the wonder young audiences feel today watching Chris Reeve or Henry Cavill fly, and even in ways possibly overlooked. Donenfeld and Liebowitz—like Siegel and Shuster—are long since gone from this world, but they gave back probably a lot more than many of *today's* business titans. Harry Donenfeld was a founder of the Albert Einstein College of Medicine in New York, which is renown for its work in genetics, cancer, diabetes, AIDS, and women's health. Jack Liebowitz was a founding trustee and board member of the North Shore-Long Island Jewish Health System, which includes a nationally distinguished children's hospital. Those millions of dimes did a lot of good work."

"As my late mother was fond of saying, 'We'll get our reward in the next world, *not* this one.' Having just turned 60, I'm coming to believe this as well. And I believe that Jerry and Joe *are* in that next world—along with George Reeves—all born a century ago, passed on, and now fully enjoying all of the good karma—here in this room and all around the world—generated by the creative brilliance they put into Superman. Outside of this room, I'm not too sure how many people would recognize the names of Messrs. Donenfeld and Liebowitz, but *Jerry Siegel and Joe Shuster* are now part of the credits of every Superman film, television series, and comic book sold today. It could just be *they're* the ones holding all the marbles now."

That Marvelous Privilege

There was one more speaker at Super Celebration 2014 that afternoon that isn't listed above. He wasn't even present; I spoke his words for him, which were given to me by his friend, Toni VallesKey Collins. His name was Bob Holiday, star of the 1966 Broadway musical *"It's a Bird...It's a Plane...It's Superman"* (see Chapter Eleven). And here's what he wrote:

"A big hello to everyone gathered out there in California. I wish I could be there with you for these three great guys, Jerry, Joe, and George. I have some history with these three. I grew up reading *Superman* comics and for that I owe Jerry and Joe *big-time*. Superman was *my* hero. Then I got the chance to *be* Superman. My Mom told me she knew I'd do a good job with the part because I always read *Superman* comics. And that was Jerry and Joe. They made me want to *be* Superman."

"Getting ready to be Superman, I got to meet Joe Shuster at the DC Comics studio. He gave me some ideas about how to make myself into Superman, and he sent me a Happy New Year card that year. I still have it. And I watched the George Reeves TV shows. I hadn't always seen them the first time around because I was working, but I didn't know then that someday I would *share* that marvelous privilege that one day *I* would be Superman *too*. So I watched reruns to get ready for the part. George meant a *lot* to me. Being Superman gets into your blood. It changes you as a man and lives with you for the rest of your life. It's good to know that there are longtime loyal George Reeves fans gathered here today. Thanks for letting me be part of this, and let me say this one more time: '*Up, up, and away!*'"

Fond Memories

There were many memorable moments at Super Celebration 2014. They included seeing Jack Larson reconnect with and embrace John Hamilton, Jr. for the first time in 60 years. We learned that George Reeves had planned to establish a college tuition fund for the son of single-parent Perry White actor John Hamilton, but this never happened due to Reeves' untimely death. There was the showing of *Jimmy!*, dedicated fan Brad Shey's inspired video compilation of *Adventures of Superman* scenes featuring Jack Larson's famous *Daily Planet* cub reporter. There was also a group tour on the following day of the Pasadena Playhouse, where George Reeves learned to act and frequently performed on the stage from 1935 until 1953. His Pasadena Playhouse colleagues included a who's who of midcentury Hollywood talent, including Gig Young, Raymond Burr, Robert Taylor, Dana Andrews, Robert Preston, and many others. Afterwards many folks in the tour group drove over to George Reeves' former residence at 1579 Benedict Canyon Drive, in Beverly Hills to pay their respects.

"George Reeves was special to many people who grew up in the 1950s," noted Jim Nolt in a Lancaster PA newspaper article published a few weeks after Super Celebration 2014. "He had a warm and generous nature that was clearly evident in his interpretation of the characters of both Clark Kent and Superman. I hope you all leave here today with some new friends and some very fond memories."

We did, Jim, thanks to you!

Chapter Fourteen

Unsung Heroes

Two of the most successful Superman media adaptations have been his syndicated newspaper strip and network radio serial. During their heights of popularity both had massive audiences, including a percentage of adults. Distributed by the McClure syndicate, the Superman strip premiered in daily newspapers on January 16, 1939 and in Sunday newspapers on November 5, 1939. The strip ran until May of 1966. During the 1940s *Superman* appeared in more than 300 daily newspapers and 90 Sunday editions, with a readership of over 20 million. *The Adventures of Superman* radio program, meanwhile, aired nationwide from 1940 to 1951, and for much of its history was sponsored by Kellogg's PEP cereal and broadcast by the Mutual Radio Network as a 15-minute Monday-to-Friday after-school serial with story arcs lasting several days or longer. A March 3, 1947 article in *The New Republic* listed *Superman*'s weekly radio listenership at 4.5 million. Each adaptation also made headlines on at least one occasion during their histories.

The August 20, 1945 issues of both *TIME* and *Newsweek* magazines reported that four months earlier the FBI had ordered Superman Inc. to discontinue a newspaper-strip story referencing atom-smashers. Nuclear research was top-secret prior to the August 6th and 9th bombings of Hiroshima and Nagasaki that ended World War II. The writers of the syndicated Superman newspaper strip, however, had been developing a plotline based on this cutting-edge scientific research. The government censored it.

On April 29, 1946 *Newsweek* reported, "*Superman* is the first children's [radio] program to develop a social consciousness. The first sequence involves Superman with a tough bunch of young intolerants who gang up on an effort to establish an Inter-Faith Community House. For moral assistance, Superman is supplied with a Catholic priest of the Crosby-Father O'Malley type and a young Jewish rabbi, a former lightweight boxer at his seminary. Currently Robert Maxwell, radio director of Superman Inc., feels he has won a strong point. 'Tolerance is rampant in Battle Creek,' he says. 'Every bit of PEP in Rice Krispies is tolerant.'" Other *Superman* radio continuities took on the KKK and Marshall Plan foes.

Lost Episodes

Given the popularity and historic importance of Superman's newspaper and radio exploits, one would think that these adventures would be lovingly preserved in a climate-controlled archive somewhere in deference to their respective places in American pop culture. After all, this character still entertains—and earns—millions on television's *Superman & Lois* and in other current adaptations. One would be wrong, however, to assume this.

Original art for the Superman newspaper strip was not routinely saved, but in fact discarded. Perhaps DC Comics thought the McClure Syndicate was archiving these materials and vice-versa, but the truth was that neither party saved anything. *The Adventures of Superman* radio serial, meanwhile, was recorded daily onto brittle transcription discs that were later warehoused in Brooklyn. Occasional mishandling of these discs over the decades rendered many into smashed-up bits of black plastic, their original recordings and voice-artist performances lost forever. Many of the later radio episodes are known only by their titles, with even the original scripts no longer extant.

Amazingly enough, however, large portions of the 29-year run of the Superman newspaper strip and hundreds of Superman radio serial episodes are available today for your enjoyment. Both The Kitchen Sink Press and IDW/The Library of American Comics have issued multiple reprint editions of the Superman newspaper strip, organized by different eras (e.g., *Superman: The Golden Age Dailies, The Silver Age Dailies, Superman Silver Age Sundays, Superman: The Atomic Age Sundays*, etc.). At around the same time (1997), the first digitized copies of *The Adventures of Superman* radio series began being released on CD by Radio Spirits and the Smithsonian Institution Press.

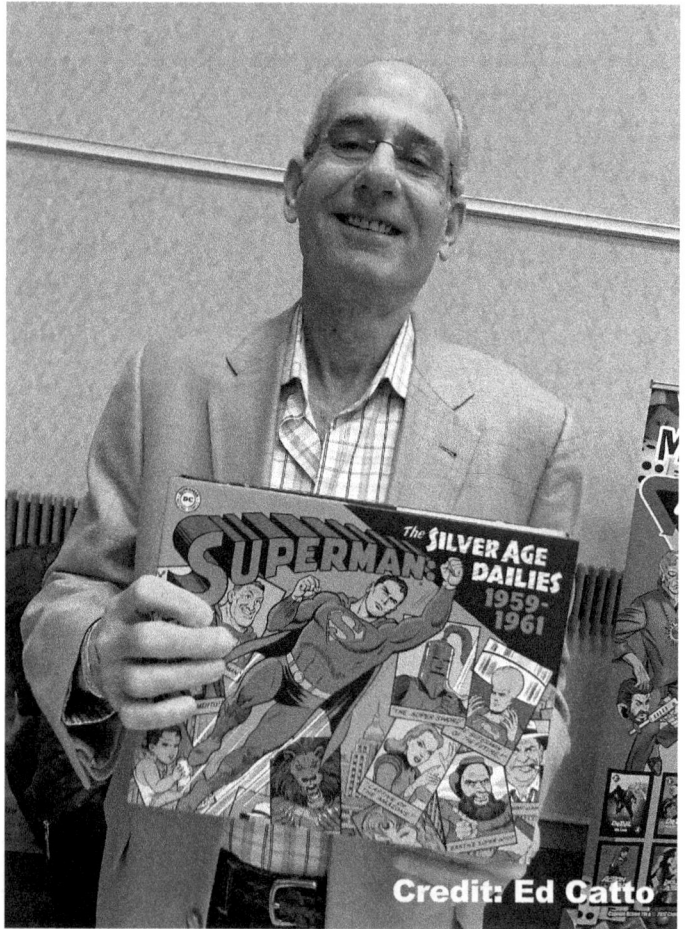

Sidney Friedfertig

Both of these re-issue series were released in cooperation with DC Comics, Superman's owner.

But if the newspaper strip was never archived and the radio series was trapped within the grooves of obsolete and often damaged 1940s electronic transcription discs in a dusty warehouse, how could they ever have been re-released in pristine new editions? The answer is through the efforts of dedicated preservationists such as Sidney Friedfertig and

Frederick W. Shay. Their stories deserve to be told and their contributions to Superman's media history deserve acknowledgment.

Origin of a Quest

"When I was a boy in the late 1950s, DC's go-to cover artist was fan favorite Curt Swan," recalls researcher/archivist Sidney Friedfertig. "His depiction of Superman, with his lithe muscular body and friendly open face, was to me the definitive version. I believed that a man could fly. But often the cover story was drawn by another, albeit great, artist and I was disappointed.

When I got older and started attending Comic Cons I sometimes spotted yellowing, Superman comic strips with Swan art for sale. It didn't take long to realize that here were the stories that matched the covers. My motivation was simple: I wanted to read and see these Swan stories. But they were not available anywhere. I once approached former DC Comics president and publisher Paul Levitz and asked about them; he replied 'We don't have them.' "

"For some reason DC decided to treat the strips like yesterday's news," Friedfertig continues. "They threw them away. More than 8,000 pieces of art and writing by the greats of comics were destroyed. There is no better example of this than the so-called 'Superman half strips.' Many years ago a young apprentice artist at DC spotted a handful of Superman dailies in the trash and rescued them. They were, unfortunately, torn in half. They are some of the few remaining original Superman dailies from the era. I decided to try to find these dailies."

"I was moderately successful," Friedfertig reveals. "Sometimes I found a month here, a week there. The Internet made my reach wider and a number of years ago I made an acquisition that gave me 97 percent of the final *six years* of dailies. These were the most elusive because by the end of the run there were fewer and fewer newspapers that carried the strip. I knew that the comic world wanted to read these so I created a web site and put them online. It received a lot of attention. Dean Mullaney, creative director of the Library of American Comics, contacted me and asked if he could publish my web site. We have been working together ever since. To be clear, these dailies have always been available to read in libraries but the microfiche is not close enough to being the quality necessary for reprinting. You must have the original dailies, or proof sheets. The challenges to finding them are many. The strips simply do not exist. I have the only known collection of dailies. It's my life's dream to see the publication of the entire run of the Superman newspaper strip."

Missing History

"In 1950 DC hired a man named Carroll Rheinstrom, president of McFadden Publications International, to travel the world selling reprint rights to the strips in foreign markets," Friedfertig explains. "He was very successful. So much so that when DC celebrated its fiftieth anniversary with the publication of the *Fifty Who Made DC Great* special edition comic book, he was an honoree. The strips were reprinted, either in digest form or in tabloids all over the globe. I have established contacts in many countries that have been very helpful. I own many episodes in foreign languages, which, if ultimately needed as our source material, will require translating. Only Britain and Australia were in English. One of my favorite memories is searching through a 150-year-old bookstore in Lisbon for Portuguese digests. Many countries also altered the strips by combining some panels, dropping or lengthening others, and adding word balloons to bridge gaps. When the Australian *Sydney Morning Herald* reprinted Wayne Boring's Superman origin story, which took up nine weeks of U.S. Sundays, they reprinted it faithfully. When the story appeared later in the Australian digest *Argus Weekly*, the nine pages of paid-for content was stretched to twelve weeks of billable content."

"This research is very satisfying," Friedfertig confides. "Comic book industry titans have told me how important my work is. It's a privilege to be the first person to publish Superman creator Jerry Siegel's final Superman work, unread since the day those strips appeared in a daily newspaper. It's recognized that Siegel, like a fine wine, improved as he aged. I liken it to the situation that would exist if the only evidence of a particular Shakespeare drama was an original playbill; unless you had a matinee ticket to the Globe theater in the year 1602 you would never have seen or heard the magic."

"When you think about all the lost history contained in these strips, however, it's upsetting," Friedfertig admits. "It's almost a crime that they were discarded without even so much as a copy made. Every daily had an individual title, and they're now lost. Mr. Mxyzptlk, Titano the Super Ape, mischievous twins Zigi and Zagi, and Superman's first love Lyla Lerroll all premiered in the strips. As of this date fans have not read the first appearances of Bizarro, Metallo, and Brainiac because they made their debuts in the strips — all scripted by Jerry Siegel. Superman had a wife and family in 1951 in the dailies, for two years of stories that fans have still not read! The only Superman strip ever censored [referenced earlier] appeared in the dailies. And of course there is the legendary Steve Allen continuity."

This 1955 story arc featuring the co-creator and first host of NBC's *Tonight Show* is among the strip's most legendary, with an entire generation of aging Allen fans still clamoring to read it. Written by DC managing editor Jack Schiff, it has yet to be reprinted in its entirety. Allen, who wore glasses and bore a close resemblance to everyone's concept of Clark Kent, was a major Superman fan, and appeared as the character in skits on his *Steve Allen Show* and in a 1966 episode of *I've Got a Secret* with Bob Holiday (star of the Broadway musical *"It's a Bird...It's a Plane...It's Superman"*) in which Allen is hung from wires and taught how to "fly." Superman is also a key theme in Allen's 1990 novel *Murder in Manhattan*.

In addition to enjoying "lost episodes" of Superman's adventures, fans appreciate the unique artistic advantages that the newspaper strip had over the comic books. Newspaper continuities ran for many weeks, as opposed to just a few comic book pages. This allowed the artists (including such greats as Stan Kaye, Wayne Boring, Win Mortimer, and — of course — Curt Swan) greater creative "real estate" to depict the action using innovative—and often more artistic—angles and dramatic points of view. As a result, the Superman newspaper strip often had an almost cinematic look to it, which was necessary for capturing the attention of its mostly adult readership; kids didn't buy newspapers, adults did.

Friedfertig's quest continues, as he is still seeking original newspaper printings of still-missing dates of the Superman newspaper strip. Nevertheless, Man of Steel aficionados and completists have him to thank in large measure for the extraordinary lengths he has gone to find these lost illustrated adventures and make them available to fans of all ages via caring publishers.

Radio Revival

Credit: Carol Shay

Fred Shay

Frederick W. Shay had just returned to his New Jersey home after work one afternoon in 1976 when his wife turned on the radio expecting to hear Bob & Ray on WOR. Instead a vintage *Lone Ranger* episode was on the air. The station was replaying classic radio serials for America's bicentennial. The show had been produced decades earlier at Mutual Radio, a network WOR co-created in 1934 with Chicago's WLS and Cincinnati's WLW. Like the *Adventures of Superman*, the series was produced at WOR/Mutual headquarters at 1440 Broadway for most of its run, and the station's archives still had a few transcriptions discs in storage.

"That started me off on the whole thing," Shay recalls. A fan of Golden Age radio since childhood and an avid collector of classic broadcasts, Shay retired from his job as a draftsman the following year and became the curator of The National Broadcaster's Hall of Fame, in Wall Township, New Jersey after donating his collection of 25,000 classic radio shows to the organization's Antique Radio Club museum.

Founded by newspaper publisher Arthur S. Schreiber in 1977, over the years the Hall of Fame inducted such greats as radio's inventor Guglielmo Marconi, superstars Jack Benny, Bob Hope, and Eddie Cantor, industry titans David Sarnoff and William S. Paley, actress Celeste Holm, and New Jersey's own Frank Sinatra. Today the Hall of Fame and museum are part of The Information Age Learning Center, in Wall.

Clicks and *Pops*

Looking to further expand the museum's audio archives, Shay had heard in 1976 that DC Comics stored its historic 1940s *Adventures of Superman* radio serials in a Brooklyn warehouse. Concerned that show's thousands of vintage 16-inch "electrical transcription" recording discs might end up forgotten and discarded, he contacted DC Comics and received a positive response.

"It was 1977, and I asked DC's president at the time if he'd like to get the company's *Superman* radio transcription discs transferred to tape,"

Shay explains. "I travelled into New York and they gave me two of them. I brought the discs home and transferred them to reel-to-reel tape on my equipment, which included a heavy cast-aluminum-alloy transcription turntable originally designed for use by radio stations in the 1940s. The recordings turned out wonderful, quality-wise. Satisfied with my results, DC then told me to come to their Brooklyn warehouse. Once there, I observed workers bringing out big boxes containing probably 25 or 30 discs in a box. But then I saw them *drop* the boxes on the concrete loading dock! This broke one to two discs on each side of each box! Some of those warehouse guys looked pretty tough, so I didn't say anything."

Distraught over the condition of many of these brittle one-sided vintage discs, Shay meticulously pieced as many as he could back together with adhesive tape at his home studio and then carefully placed them on his special turntable. "It was so solid that there was no rumble in it like you'd get with a consumer turntable made for LP record albums," he notes.

To further enhance the audio quality he coated each disc with a special liquid to reduce surface noise. "It was a mixture of dishwashing liquid and something else that I don't remember now. It took a lot of the scratches and *hiss* out right from the start." Although today's sophisticated digital noise-removal software didn't exist in 1977, Shay was able to employ an early "de-clicker" device to eliminate most of the remaining *pops* that occurred when the turntable tone arm's stylus hit an especially bad crack. "After I put them through it you'd never know there was anything wrong with the discs," he says of his restoration. "There were about 100 shows where the discs were broken and had to be put back together again, but in the end I did well over 350 shows. It was a job to do it; hundreds of hours of audio material transferred to tape. I wore earphones while restoring it all, and as a result I've had a ringing in my ears—tinnitus—ever since."

Twenty Years After

Shay's dedication to preserving radio's *Adventures of Superman* also required him to use his own car to transport the boxes of heavy discs from the Brooklyn warehouse to his New Jersey home studio and back. This unfortunately included getting sideswiped by a hit-and-run taxi. But most disappointing of all was DC's decision on what to do with the tapes he created of the transferred radio episodes. "The stipulation was that nothing was going to be done with them," he reveals. "I think they wanted to wait till everybody associated with the show passed away before putting them out."

Consumer electronics manufacturers, however, had their own plans. Sony's introduction of the Walkman in the early 1980s made on-the-go listening to music, books on tape, lectures, and—yes—old-time radio shows on audiocassettes convenient and irresistible to millions. The introduction of the Compact Disc (CD) a few years later further increased the popularity of portable audio programming for everyone from joggers to airline passengers to motorists. This expanding market for prerecorded audio content prompted renewed interest in old-time radio, with companies such as Radio Spirits releasing restored copies of such classics as the original *Dragnet*, *Gunsmoke*, and *The Jack Benny Program* on audiocassettes and CDs. Still among the most popular fictional characters ever created, Superman's entry into this audio arena was inevitable. Radio Spirits released its first Superman CD box set in 1997, in association with The Smithsonian Institution Press and DC Comics, which fortunately still had Shay's reel-to-reel transfers. Additional volumes followed, all taking advantage of the massive storage capacity of CDs to hold many episodes.

"They are beautiful editions," Shay notes. Each one included a 60-page booklet featuring detailed background information by radio historian Anthony Tollin. The booklets include rare photographs, complete cast lists, original broadcast dates, and notations of all the folks responsible for the reissues. "All pretty good except my name was never mentioned! That's the kind of luck I've had with these."

Lost and Found

Although Shay rescued and restored hundreds of hours of *Adventures of Superman* radio episodes, many others will remain lost forever. "When the war was over in 1945 they apparently took all the episodes with Japanese references and dumped them," Shay reveals. "That's why those ones don't exist. I don't know how many of them were made, but there must have been quite a few."

Among the hundreds of episodes that Shay *was* able to save, however, were numerous serialized stories dealing with ethnic and religious tolerance—an historic achievement for a program aimed at young people at a time when sensitive topics were taboo for radio. In 1949 *The Adventures of Superman* moved to ABC, with actor Michael Fitzmaurice taking over from Bud Collyer and announcer Ross Martin (future co-star of television's *The Wild, Wild West* from 1965-69) replacing narrator Jackson Beck. Those episodes expanded to fully self-contained half-hours. "I found about 20 of those," Shay recalls. "They were in pieces, but I was able to put them together. They included the historic episode 'The Story of Marina Baum.'"

Broadcast on November 23, 1950 (the day before Thanksgiving), "The Story of Marina Baum" tells a tale in flashback of a young Polish war orphan whose family was murdered by the Nazis. The versatile Ross Martin not only narrates, but also portrays Marina's father and an elderly woodcutter who hides Marina in a convent. Later, living in Metropolis USA, the girl finds herself yet again the victim of "the insidious forces of rumor and suspicion," as narrator Martin intones.

Clark Kent receives a call from Jimmy Olsen's mother, frantic that her son was in trouble for beating a bigoted boy who said "awful things to Marina." Quickly changing into Superman, a few visits from the Man of Steel—assisted by sympathetic neighborhood priest Father Damien—resolves the situation, with Jimmy no longer in trouble and the bully's father agreeing that his son deserved the thrashing. All then join together to celebrate Thanksgiving 1950.

The episode ends with a reminder to see the new *Atom Man Vs. Superman* movie serial at local theaters—ironic not only because it was partially inspired by an *Adventures of Superman* radio continuity, but because years later Shay became friends with Superman serial star Kirk Alyn, and helped "pester" DC Comics to convince Warner Home Video to release the popular serial on VHS tape in 1988.

Given the popularity and subject matter of Superman's long-running radio *and* newspaper exploits, it's safe to say that both versions entertained millions and had a positive impact on society. Their success led to subsequent Superman media incarnations in movie serials, television, Broadway, and feature films. Thanks to the efforts of Frederick W. Shay and Sidney Friedfertig, this historic content was saved from oblivion and is now available for our appreciation and study. Both of these gentlemen deserve our super-thanks.

Chapter Fifteen

Super Music

Quick, answer this question: What do Taylor Swift, Bon Jovi, Alanis Morissette, Eric Clapton, Willie Nelson, The Commodores, Keith Urban, Barbra Streisand, the Atlanta Rhythm Section, Kenny Rogers, Celine Dion, and Don McLean all have in common?

They've all recorded (and in many cases written) original songs inspired by Superman. These aren't songs created for use in a Superman film or a television series; these are standalone compositions that tell a story or express ideas using Superman as a central metaphor. Each one is different. Many use the word *Superman* in the title. And in addition to the dozen songs listed above, there are more than 100 others (and that's not even counting tunes in which Superman is limited to a passing mention, such as Jim Croce's 1972 hit "You Don't Mess Around With Jim" or "Land of Confusion" by Genesis, in 1986).

Although one might naturally think of John Williams' instantly recognizable *Superman: The Movie* march or the Hans Zimmer *Man of Steel* theme when one hears the phrase *Superman music*, the character's musical heritage predates and extends far beyond movies and television, and includes scores of songs and instrumentals in practically every genre, from rock, to jazz, to country, and beyond. There's even a *Metropolis Symphony*, five *Superman* comics-inspired movements by pianist Michael Daugherty composed from 1988-1993. And don't forget *"It's a Bird...It's a Plane...It's Superman,"* the 1966 Hal Prince Broadway musical by composer Charles Strouse and lyricist Lee Adams. Considered collectively, Superman-inspired popular music is yet another

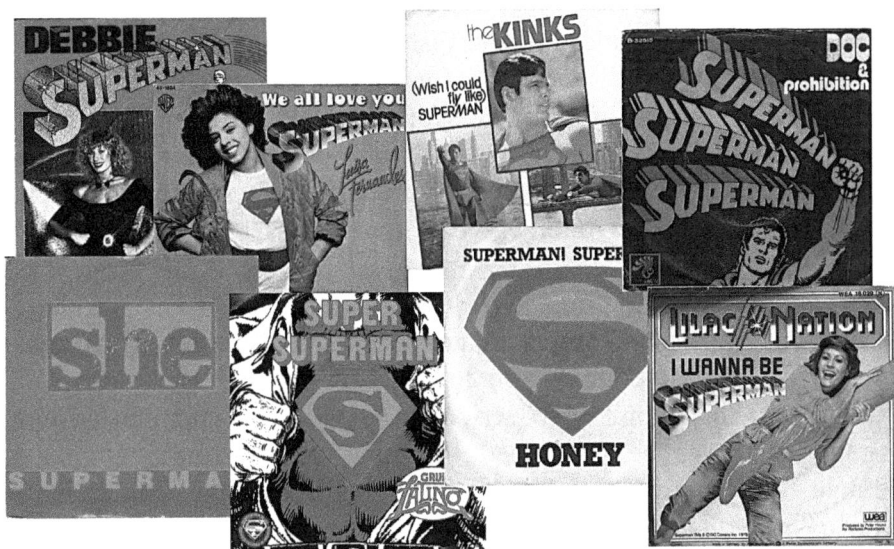

Many musical genres, one inspiration.

unique, perhaps astonishing, aspect that sets this character apart from all others.

The Countdown Begins

Superman's pop music career got off to an auspicious start in 1940 with a fox trot recorded by no less than the King of Swing himself, Benny Goodman. Perhaps it's appropriate that the Man of Steel's first record should be a jazz number, jazz and comic books being two American-born art forms originally regarded by many as "disreputable" but soon loved and emulated the world over. This one-word-titled hit was written and arranged by jazzman Eddie Sauter, who would later not only co-lead the Sauter-Finegan Orchestra, but also create innovative orchestrations for *"It's a Bird...It's a Plane...It's Superman"* on Broadway in 1966.

One month before Fleischer Studios composer Sammy Timberg unleashed his rousing "Superman March" upon the public in the first Paramount Superman theatrical cartoon (a 1941 theme that was later played on an organ to herald the start of nearly every Superman radio serial episode), bandleader Freddie Fisher and Superman radio producer Robert "Bob" Maxwell released a Decca 78 rpm novelty record titled "Superman," a bizarre little ditty performed by Freddie "Schnickelfritz" Fisher and His Orchestra. The word *schnickelfritz* means "mischievous little boy" in German. The song itself is like hearing Spike Jones on a bender. Do yourself a favor and give this one a pass.

Superman flew back to birdland in 1946 when trumpeter Pete Candoli — nicknamed "Superman" by bandmates for his ability to hit high notes — penned an original composition titled (you guessed it) "Superman." Candoli took his moniker so seriously he wore a Superman costume onstage whenever he performed the song as a member of Woody Herman's First Herd. The following year The Miles Davis Quintet issued its own "Superman" jazz instrumental, this one written by Davis himself.

Superman music diversified in the 1950s, with rockabilly singer Dale Hawkins and blues pianist Stomp Gordon releasing "Superman" and "Ride, Superman, Ride," respectively, in 1956. Folk singer Tom Glazer's 1959 "Superman" song is yet another original composition with that title; the tune was re-released many times on children's records in the years to follow. No doubt there were other Superman-inspired recordings during that decade of early rock & roll just waiting for a keen researcher to discover. Of course, the music most associated with the character at that time was the title theme to television's *Adventures of Superman*, credited to music editor Leon Klatzkin.

The list of Superman songs grew longer in the 1960s, with "(He's My) Superman" (The Sweethearts, 1962), "Superman Lover" (Andy & The Marglows, 1963), "Doin' the Superman" (Dennis & The Supertones, 1963), "Superman" (Joyce Davis, 1964), "It's Superman" (a cover from Broadway's *"It's a Bird...It's a Plane...It's Superman"* by celebrity scions Dino, Desi & Billy, 1966), two *different* songs titled "Superman" on the same album by The Hesitations (1967), and "Superman" by The New Riders of the Purple Sage, which at that point in its history was comprised of future members of The Grateful Dead. The 1960's biggest super-hit, however, was Donovan's psychedelic folk tune "Sunshine

Superman," released in 1966 and also the title of the album it's included on. The album was Donovan's most successful, peaking at number eleven in the U.S. and remaining on the *Billboard* Top LPs chart for six months. Years later the song and its title would be re-used for the 2008 documentary *Sunshine Superman: The Journey of Donovan* and a 2014 documentary about base jumpers Carl and Jean Boenish.

Off the Charts

During the 1970s the number of Superman-inspired songs continued to proliferate. To list and describe them all—and the others that have followed up to the present day—would require a book the size of the one you're reading now. A notable example of such songs during this decade is Barbra Streisand's 1977 "Superman," which was both the name of a single and the album it was released on. *Superman* the LP peaked at number three on the Top 200 LP *Billboard* album chart and has since sold two million copies in the U.S. The cover features an alluring Streisand wearing a Superman t-shirt. Another chart-topper was The Kinks' "(Wish I Could Fly Like) Superman," released in 1979 after *Superman: The Movie* became a massive hit. Featuring a disco beat, it became the anthem for Clark Kents everywhere.

Superman-inspired songs of the 1980s include Don McLean's haunting ballad "Superman's Ghost' (1987), which purports to tell the story of George Reeves' death. It includes several inaccuracies, including the line that Reeves performed Superman "live, not on tape," and that the show was due to be cancelled. Despite the artistic license it's a powerful and interesting tribute to the Superman of the Boomer generation.

Unfulfilled Dream

With so much Superman-inspired original music in existence I put together a demo CD in 1991 and sent it to Rhino Records, assuming their appreciation for quirky song collections made this a natural for them. I even offered to write the liner notes. After all, they had released two volumes of baseball songs and an album containing a dozen different versions of "Louie Louie." I wrote to their director of A&R (artists and repertoire) at the time, urging them to release a Superman song-compilation CD. I closed my letter with, "If you can release *The Best of Slim Whitman* you've got *no* excuse for not doing Superman!"

To his credit, the A&R director left a message on my answering machine saying he liked the idea of a Superman-inspired compilation, but that my idea was shot down by Rhino because licensing such a "various artists" collection was too much of a risk. (*Yes, but this is Superman*, I thought to myself. *I wonder how many Slim Whitman CDs they actually sold!*)

Years later I sort of got my wish when Rhino released *The Sound of Superman* in 2006, a collection of covers by obscure bands and other songs written for the CD. Only four had *Superman* in the title, and even Remy Zero's "Save Me" *Smallville* title track was by a cover band. The *Smallville Talon Mix* (2003) and *Metropolis Mix* (2005) were not much better. To this day, there's still no CD collection that has gathered such great tunes as Les Variations' "Superman Superman" (1975), Johnny Guitar Watson's "Superman Lover" (1976), or The Spin Doctors' "Jimmy Olsen's Blues" (1991). Perhaps some enterprising music label may yet eventually step-up and put such a collection together.

The Superman hits, however, just keep on coming. Do a search and you can build an incredible super-playlist. No other comic book character has inspired so much music. But one should expect nothing less of Superman.

Chapter Sixteen

Ten Reasons Why Superman is The Best

Superlatives are risky. "The first," "the best," "the greatest," and similar designations are always subject to challenges. People have loved make-believe heroes since *The Epic of Gilgamesh* 4,000 years ago. He probably had antecedents too. The 1930s brought us Philip Wylie's *Gladiator* and such characters as Doc Savage, Flash Gordon, and The Phantom (the latter two without supernatural abilities). Later decades brought us Spider-Man, who has "problems," and The Thing, who is made of rocks. All well and good.

Superman, however, is in a class by himself. His long media history is unmatched by any of his peers. Need evidence? Re-read the first Chapter, but also consider this List of Reasons, which stops at ten because this book had to end somewhere.

1- *Action Comics* **No. 1** – The birth of the superhero. Unprecedented; a cover featuring a red-caped man in a blue leotard holding up an automobile and smashing it against a boulder. It flew off newsstands in 1938. Crisp copies of this ten-cent issue now sell for more than $3 million.

2- Max Fleischer – Yes, Popeye and Betty Boop were also animated by Fleischer Studios. But not like Superman, in stylized Technicolor photorealism. Still incredible to behold.

3- *The Adventures of Superman* **radio series** – Intended for kids, it included stories that championed ethnic and religious tolerance. And this was back in the 1940s! Media references usually cite the 1946 "Clan of the Fiery Cross" continuity, but that was just one of many anti-bias scripts to be produced by this decade-long radio serial.

4- *The Adventures of Superman* **television series** – Among the first "single-camera," film-originated television series, it was the first with optically produced effects shots, and was more than a decade ahead of its time in live action. Totaling 104 episodes produced between 1951 and 1957 (the latter 52 of which were shot in color a decade before color telecasts became the norm), it was the most successful syndicated television series for many years, and it's still on television today. How many 1950s shows (other than *I Love Lucy* and *The Honeymooners*) can you say that about? Seen from today's perspective, *The Adventures of Superman* also provides an historical link between 1940's B-movie film noir and the full-color TV sci-fi that would arrive in the 1960s. (And please don't try to argue that *The Lone Ranger* and *Dick Tracy* were "superheroes." They weren't.)

5- *I Love Lucy* **episode 166, "Lucy and Superman"** – The immortal Lucille Ball and Desi Arnaz with Superman George Reeves in a 1957 episode of their television series. Other characters may be cool, but they'll never be Lucy/Desi/Reeves cool. Unique.

6- Metropolis, Illinois – "The Hometown of Superman," it features a 15-foot-tall Superman statue, The Super Museum (70,000 Superman artifacts, open year-round), and the annual Superman Celebration attracting thousands of visitors from all over the world each June. There's also a Harrah's casino and historic Fort Massac. Every Superman fan visits Metropolis at least once; many others visit it frequently.

7- *Superman vs. Muhammad Ali* **celebrity comic book (1978)** – Only one superhero could do battle with The Greatest. An all-time bestseller.

8- *Superman: the Movie* – The first megabudget superhero movie, It won a Special Achievement Oscar for Best Visual Effects and today ranks with such classics as *The Wizard of Oz*. Watching it is the first thing Marvel Studios directors do when they embark on a new film (as evidenced by their success). Christopher Reeve, Marlon Brando, Gene Hackman—combined with its sequel and adjusted for inflation, they were the first such films to earn $1 billion.

9- Seinfeld and Superman – Yadda yadda yadda.

10- Batman – He's Superman's best friend. Case closed.

Chapter Seventeen

Super Bibliography

As you should know by now, this book is a collection of 40 years of interviews and reports from my files. It is *not* a comprehensive history of Superman or the many comic book titles, television shows, movies, collectibles, etc. based on the character. There are, however, many excellent books available that *are* dedicated to such topics. Listed below are some notable examples, with a personal comment on each. Not included in these titles are all the excellent reprints of Superman comic books and newspaper strips, which are worth a lengthy Google.

Agostino, Lauren; Newberg, A.L. *Holding Kryptonite: Truth, Justice and America's First Superhero* (Holmes Watson, Armonk NY), 2014. Think you know the Siegel and Shuster story? Think again. This eye-opening book is a must-read.

Alyn, Kirk. *A Job For Superman!* (Kirk Alyn, Hollywood), 1971. The first autobiography of a Superman actor, it provides a glimpse of the bygone days of the movie serials. Copies occasionally surface on eBay.

Bettinson, Gary. *Superman: The Movie – The 40th Anniversary Interviews* (Intellect, Bristol UK), 2018. Q&A's with many of the surviving talents involved in Superman's greatest media adaptation.

Bifulco, Mike. *Superman on Television: Tenth Anniversary Edition* (Michael Bifulco, Grand Rapids MI), 1998. Long and short plot summaries of all 104 episodes of *The Adventures of Superman*, produced over six seasons from 1951-57.

Blue, Howard. *The Man Who Sold Superman to the World* (Snake Pond Press, Copake NY), 2022. How a man named Carroll Rheinstrom made DC Comics go global.

Bowers, Jim; McKernan, Brian. *Superman: The Richard Donner Years* (Jim Bowers, Las Vegas), 2015. More of a book prototype, this lavish but very limited-edition coffee table book features rare and beautiful color and B&W production stills and behind-the-scenes photos along with continuity Polaroids, contact sheets, and other seldom-seen images from this classic film.

Bowers, Rick. *Superman Versus The Ku Klux Klan* (National Geographic, Washington DC), 2012. A bit of a lost opportunity here. The book details activist Stetson Kennedy's infiltration of the KKK and *The Adventures of Superman* radio serial's efforts to use his information to discredit the organization, but it examines only one of several tolerance-oriented storylines produced during the run of this series. There were others also deserving mention, and they made this radio serial remarkable for its time.

Daniels, Les. *Superman, The Complete History: The Life and Times of the Man of Steel* (Chronicle Books, San Francisco), 1998. This nicely illustrated volume leaves you wishing it had twice as many pages and photographs. A subsequent *Superman Masterpiece Edition: The Golden Age of America's First Super Hero* included a nice Superman statuette, but it's essentially a reshuffling of the same content.

Darowski, John (editor). *The Ages of Superman* (McFarland & Co., Inc., Jefferson NC), 2012. Essays on the Man of Steel in Changing Times. The title says it all.

Darowski, John (editor). *Adapting Superman: Essays on the Transmedia Man of Steel* (McFarland & Co., Inc., Jefferson NC), 2021. A collection of academics examines the various media versions of Superman. Like the adaptations, the quality of the essays varies.

De Haven, Tom. *Our Hero: Superman on Earth* (Yale University Press, New Haven CT), 2010. The author wrote the novel *It's Superman!* five years earlier and followed up with this book-length essay. Both are well worth your time.

Dooley, Dennis; Engle, Gary (editors). *Superman at Fifty! The Persistence of a Legend!* (Octavia, Cleveland OH), 1987. DC Comics took me out to lunch in 1985 after an agent sent them my book proposal titled *Superman at Fifty: The Golden Anniversary of the Man of Steel.* They published this book instead. Wise move. Contributors include Curt Swan, Dennis O'Neil, Harvey Pekar (and others), *and* Harlan Ellison's magnificent Superman quote adorns the back cover. This deserves a place on your shelf.

Galloway, John T. *The Gospel According to Superman* (A.J. Holman Co., Philadelphia and New York), 1973. The first (but not the last) book written about Superman and religion.

Grossman, Gary. *Superman: Serial to Cereal* (Popular Library, Big Apple Film Series, New York), 1976. This volume was the first to catapult Superman television and movie fandom out of its comic book origins and into the mainstream media. All the other books in this bibliography are its descendants. Bravo, Mr. Grossman!

Harter, Chuck. *Superboy and Superpup: The Lost Videos* (Cult Movie Press, Hollywood), 1993. The full story behind two failed television pilots produced after the death of George Reeves.

Hayde, Michael J. *Flights of Fantasy* (BearManor Media, Albany GA), 2009. A super achievement. Hayde's meticulous research delivers a vivid history of the talents and era that spawned a leading golden age radio serial and its transition into an historic filmed television series that became one of the medium's most successful programs.

Henderson, Jan Allen. *Speeding Bullet: The Life and Bizarre Death of George Reeves* (Michael Bifulco, Grand Rapids MI) 1999. For those wishing to descend into the rabbit hole of George Reeves' death, this is one place to start.

Holiday, Bob; Harter, Chuck. *Superman on Broadway* (Bob Holiday & Chuck Harter, Hawley PA), 2003. An entertaining biography of the titular star of the 1966 Hal Prince musical comedy *"It's a Bird...It's a Plane...It's Superman"* (see Chapter Eleven).

Kashner, Sam and Schoenberger, Nancy. *Hollywood Kryptonite* (St. Martin's Press, New York), 1996. Disliked by some, this examination of George Reeves' death inspired the 2006 film *Hollywoodland*.

Levitz, Paul. *The Little Book of Superman* (Taschen, New York), 2015. This is a pocket-size digest of Levitz's mammoth *75 Years of DC Comics: The Art of Modern Mythmaking*, published in 2010.

Matetsky, Harry; Amanda Murrah Matetsky; Fuchs, Danny. *The Adventures of Superman Collecting* (Russ Cochran, West Plains MO), 1988. This beautiful slipcase edition coffee table book features more than 500 significant Superman items photographed in full color, and printed as a limited run of 2,500 copies.

Peretti, Daniel. *Superman in Myth and Folklore* (University Press of Mississippi, Jackson MS), 2017. A well-written analysis of the deep connection fans have for Superman.

Petrou, David Michael. *The Making of Superman: The Movie* (Warner Books, New York), 1978. The best making-of book ever written, according to Steven Spielberg.

Reeve, Dana. *Care Packages: Letters to Christopher Reeve from Strangers and Other Friends* (Random House, New York), 1999. A testament to how deeply loved this greatest of all Superman actors was.

Ricca, Brad. *Super Boys* (St. Martin's Press, New York), 2013. The biography of Superman creators Jerry Siegel and Joe Shuster, detailed and thorough.

Rossen, Jake. *Superman vs. Hollywood: How Fiendish Producers, Devious Directors, and Warring Writers Grounded an American Icon* (Chicago Review Press, Chicago), 2008. A well-researched report on Hollywood's inability to come to grips with the fact that Richard Donner's *Superman: The Movie* will never be surpassed.

Scivally, Bruce. *Superman on Film, Television, Radio and Broadway* (McFarland & Co., Inc., Jefferson NC), 2008. An excellent history of Superman's life beyond print.

Superman Returns: The Official Movie Guide (Time Inc. Home Entertainment, New York), 1976. Nice color photos from a disappointing movie.

Tye, Larry. *Superman: The High-Flying History of America's Most Enduring Hero* (Random House, New York), 2012. The best Superman biography (and not just because my name is in it four times).

Ward, Larry Thomas. *Truth, Justice, & The American Way: The Life and Times of Noel Neill—The Original Lois Lane* (Nicholas Lawrence Books, Los Angeles), 2003. A charming biography of "First Lady of Metropolis" Noel Neill, the original live-action Lois Lane in the 1948 and 1950 Superman movie serials and in 78 episodes of *The Adventures of Superman* television series. An expanded collector's edition is also available with more photos and color.

Weldon, Glen. *Superman: The Unauthorized Biography* (Wiley, Hoboken NJ), 2013. Only a character with a long and fascinating history could sustain multiple high-quality biographies. This is one of them.

White, John Wesley. *The Man From Krypton: The Gospel According to Superman* (Bethany Fellowship, Minneapolis MN), 1978. Superman and religion again.

White, Mark D. (editor); Irwin, William (series editor). *Superman and Philosophy: What Would The Man of Steel Do?* (Wiley-Blackwell, Chichester, West Sussex UK), 2013. A deep dive into Superman morality starting with Nietzsche.

Wolverton, Mark; Stern, Roger (editor). *The Science of Superman* (ibooks, New York), 2002. Could Superman's powers have any basis in fact? A surprising analysis.

Yeffeth, Glenn (editor). *The Man From Krypton* (Benbella Books, Inc., Dallas), 2005. Just when you thought you'd read every possible "take" on Superman, here's a collection of 20 more thought-provoking commentaries.

About the Author

Brian McKernan is an audiobook narrator/voiceover artist and a retired PR writer and editor of trade magazines covering broadcast, teleproduction, and cinema technologies. He credits Superman/DC comic books with learning to read and his love for the printed word. He has also written *Digital Cinema: The Revolution in Cinematography, Postproduction, and Distribution* (McGraw Hill, 2005) and *Superman: The Richard Donner Years* (with Jim Bowers, 2015). He is the editor of *Creating Digital Content* (with John Rice; McGraw Hill, 2002), *Producer to Producer* (by Michael Wiese; Michael Wiese Productions, 1997), and *The Age of Videography* (Miller Freeman PSN, 1996). He is also the co-producer of the video documentary *Holiday in Metropolis* and the creator of the *Superman in Advertising & Media* Facebook group. He lives in Westchester County, New York.

www.ingramcontent.com/pod-product-compliance
Lightning Source LLC
Chambersburg PA
CBHW052002090426
42741CB00008B/1512